SHORT WAL...

Shropshire Pubs

Robert Smart

COUNTRYSIDE BOOKS
NEWBURY, BERKSHIRE

COUNTRYSIDE BOOKS
3 Catherine Road
Newbury, Berkshire

ISBN 1 85306 358 4

Designed by Mon Mohan
Cover illustration by Colin Doggett

Produced through MRM Associates Ltd., Reading
Typeset by Paragon Typesetters, Queensferry, Clwyd
Printed in Great Britain by J W Arrowsmith Ltd, Bristol

Contents

Publisher's Note

We hope that you obtain considerable enjoyment from this book; great care has been taken in its preparation. However, changes of landlord and actual closures are sadly not uncommon. Likewise, although at the time of publication all routes followed public rights of way or permitted paths, diversion orders can be made and permissions withdrawn.

We cannot of course be held responsible for such diversion orders and any inaccuracies in the text which result from these or any other changes to the routes, nor any damage which might result from walkers trespassing on private property. However, we are anxious that all details covering the walks and the pubs are kept up to date and would therefore welcome information from readers which would be relevant to future editions.

Area map showing locations of the walks.

Introduction

Shropshire is described in several guides as the most beautiful of English counties – and it certainly is one of the least spoilt. It is beyond the ever-stretching tentacles of the London sprawl and, although not far from the Birmingham conurbation as the crow flies, it has, apart from Telford, escaped large scale developments and remains a quiet and lovely area in which to find rest and repose.

The walks vary from the wild, windswept uplands of south Shropshire to calm canalside routes, as in north Shropshire and across the Shropshire Plain. This is certainly a county of contrasts. The southern part is dominated by the Stretton Hills, the last vestiges of the Welsh Mountains which spill over into the English border counties. The Longmynd is a mecca for all serious walkers as well as the casual rambler, while the other hills in the area offer in different ways their own particular attractions. Wenlock Edge, immortalised in song and verse, stretches north-east/south-west across the region while the Clee Hills give Shropshire the distinction of having the highest peaks south of the Pennines. The river Severn cuts the county into two and north of it we come to the Shropshire Plain, interrupted here and there by rocky outcrops such as Haughmond Hill, Harmer Hill and Grinshill. The longest stretch of any canal within a single county is to the north and affords some enjoyable walks, while the area to the south-west of the A5 around Oswestry is almost entirely untouched by the 20th century and a stroll there is rather like stepping back into a bygone age, such is the peace and tranquillity one finds.

Shrewsbury itself is a most attractive county town and even recent developments have been carried out with taste and decorum, as befits a place of its character. Being in the centre of the county, directions to the start of all walks are based on starting from there. Other market towns worthy of closer examination are Ludlow, Oswestry, Whitchurch, Much Wenlock and Market Drayton, all of which have walks near them in this book.

Points of interest along the way are also included in the text.

Public footpaths are safeguarded by law and should be signposted and clear of obstructions, which is not always the case, and any problems, such as crops (footpaths should be cleared to a width of 3 ft, bridleways to 6 ft) or bulls unattended by cows, should be reported to the County Council Leisure Services Department, Column House, Shrewsbury. Public rights of way can be waymarked in two ways, either by blue or yellow arrows, or blue or yellow tape; blue signifies a bridleway, which means the track can be used by horses as well as pedestrians, and yellow signifies access restricted to pedestrians only.

Each walk was carefully chosen, after considerable research on the basis of being suitable for families with young children, as well as anyone wanting a short ramble, so I was constantly aware of the problems nettles cause to bare young legs and mention this hazard if such is likely to occur, otherwise I hope you will find the walks give you and your companions much enjoyment.

Robert Smart
Summer 1995

① Grindley Locks near Whitchurch
The Horse and Jockey

The Horse and Jockey is a typical roadside inn. Rather too close to the town to ever have been a coaching inn it nevertheless would have been used by road and canal travellers. Built about 1780, most of it appears to be original with very little in the way of recent additions. The lounge is compact and comfortable, and some of the tables are made from old sewing machine bases. Several canalside paintings are hung on the walls along with brasses. Outside there is a large area for children, fenced off from the car park so they can play there in safety.

Hanson's Bitter, Harp lager, Banks's Bitter and Mild, Kronenbourg 1664 and Guinness are on offer, as well as Woodpecker cider. The food, which is available from 12 noon to 2 pm and 7 pm to 9 pm every day, includes hot pies, salads, ploughman's lunches, basket meals, chicken, plaice, scampi and steaks. You will also find a vegetarian menu, a children's menu and sweets. The opening hours are from 12 noon to 3 pm and 7 pm to 11 pm (10.30 pm on Sunday).

Telephone: 01948 662723.

How to get there: From Shrewsbury take the A49 north, as signposted 'Whitchurch'. On the approach to Whitchurch follow the bypass, taking the third exit left, the A41 towards Chester. The Horse and Jockey is just a few yards further.

Parking: There is a large car park at the pub.

Length of the walk: 2 miles. Map: OS Landranger 117 Chester, Wrexham and surrounding area (inn GR 521431).

The entertainment of watching the boats going up and down the flight of locks, particularly at weekends when the canal is busy, may keep you from the walk for some time. There are several seats to sit on and enjoy the canalside spectacle. When you finally set off, you will find the route easy and fairly level overall. The first half of the walk is on the canal towpath and you return to the pub on a stretch of the Shropshire Way.

The Walk

From the pub cross the busy A41 when safe to do so, into a stony track just to the left of the garage. There is a public footpath sign at the start and a notice board detailing walks along the Sandstone Trail. This trail is a long-distance footpath which begins here at Grindley and finishes at Frodsham, in Cheshire. It is 30 miles long and visits many of the sandstone outcrops which occur in that part of Cheshire, such as at Beeston Castle. Bear right by the bridge onto the towpath which will eventually take you past the locks as far as bridge 30. If you look back, to your left, you will see the canal tunnel under the embankment of the former Whitchurch/Chester railway line which crosses the canal.

Shortly after joining the canal you come to the basin at the foot of the Grindley Locks. The locks are a flight of basins by which boats ascend and descend – the notice board by the bridge shows how this works. The basins at the bottom and at the top are used as boat parks while they wait their turn. After passing under the A41 road bridge the locks ascend and on the right is the shop where canal users can replenish their supplies. Picture postcards and films are also sold here.

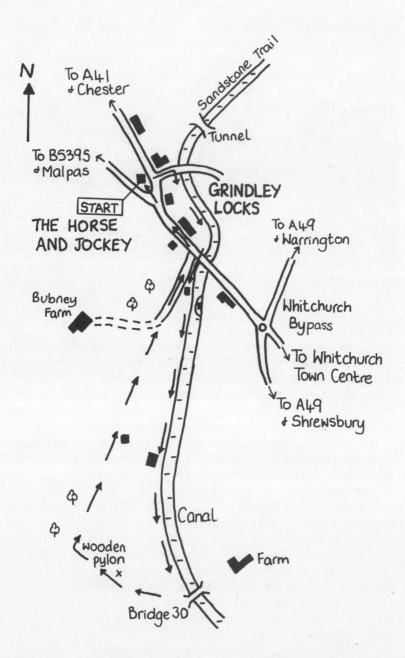

N

To A41
& Chester

Sandstone Trail

Tunnel

To B5395
& Malpas

GRINDLEY
LOCKS

START

THE HORSE
AND JOCKEY

To A49
& Warrington

Bubney
Farm

Whitchurch
Bypass

To Whitchurch
Town Centre

To A49
& Shrewsbury

Canal

Farm

wooden
pylon
x

Bridge 30

Canal locks near Whitchurch.

After passing the lock keeper's cottage at the top, the walk continues alongside the canal, passing a very isolated canalside cottage. On a quiet day you may be fortunate enough to see a heron or a kingfisher. At bridge 30, turn right over a waymarked stile and cross the first field, heading towards a stile at the foot of a wooden electricity pylon. Go straight ahead over the stile to the hedge on the far side of the field and over the gate there. Now turn right along the Shropshire Way. (Should this field path be blocked by crops, you can make use of the map to find a way round.)

Follow the Shropshire Way, marked with black and white waymarks depicting a buzzard with wings outstretched. It goes straight on, with the hedge on the right, over three stiles until, with the farmhouse near to your left, you join the farm lane. Continue to the A41 main road, and turning left you will see the Horse and Jockey just ahead of you. Do remember to look back before crossing the B5395 Malpas road as the traffic from Whitchurch sweeps round at speed.

2 Welshampton
The Sun

Between the tourist mecca of Ellesmere with its famous lake, and Whitchurch, lies the little hamlet of Welshampton, which boasts only a few cottages besides the inevitable garage, church and pub.

The inn is 18th century, built around 1770 as a farm and later a malting house. The room at the west end was until recently a butcher's shop. Children are welcome in the lounge bar, which is comfortably furnished, and outside there is a play area with swings. A good selection of beers include Greenalls Mild, Guinness, Tetley Bitter, Carling Black Label and Labatt's, and there is Strongbow cider. The menu is wide ranging and covers all tastes. Basket meals (they call them 'snacks' but they are large enough for most appetites) are available at lunchtimes, in addition to the main menu, which includes chicken, scampi, plaice, jacket potatoes, pizza and umpteen steaks, a children's menu, a vegetarian menu, starters and sweets – you certainly won't go away hungry! The opening hours on Monday to

Saturday are 12 noon to 2 pm and 7 pm to 11 pm, or all day on Saturday if occasion demands. On Sunday the times are the usual 12 noon to 3 pm and 7 pm to 10.30 pm.
Telephone: 01948 710637.

How to get there: From Shrewsbury take the A528 almost as far as Ellesmere, but at the junction with the A495 turn right onto the latter, signposted 'Whitchurch', and Welshampton is 2 miles further.

Parking: There is a large car park at the Sun.

Length of the walk: 2½ or 3 miles. Map: OS Landranger 126 Shrewsbury and surrounding area (inn GR 435350).

I like this walk enormously. It uses quiet country lanes, which seem to have been forgotten by the motor car, and a canal towpath, and is what I would call pushchair friendly. The lane from Welshampton to the canal is twisty and quiet and dotted with wild Shropshire damson trees, but alas too high to be reached when the fruit is ripe.

The Walk
From the pub car park, cross the road and take the public footpath directly opposite. It skirts the left-hand boundary of the garage and, passing the house ahead, becomes a narrow path between two hedges. Cross the first stile and continue. Turn left along the lane, which leads to the canal. There is no footpath, so care should be taken although traffic is very light.

On reaching the canal there is a way down on either side of the lane but the path to the left is easier. Turn right under the bridge and follow the towpath. The restoration of our canal system has been a great achievement as the towpaths make ideal walks.

If you wish to take the shorter walk, leave the towpath at the next bridge (52), and follow the lane, turning first right at a crossroads where it says 'Unsuitable for Motors'. This is where the longer walk rejoins.

The longer walk continues along the towpath as far as bridge 53. Immediately after bridge 52 the towpath has been restored. It had collapsed and was out of use for many years, during

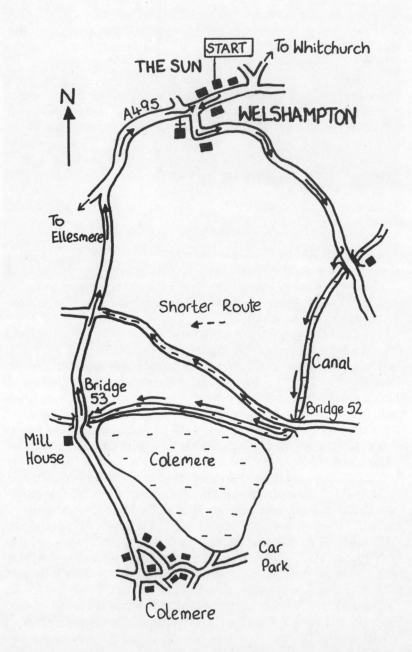

START

THE SUN

To Whitchurch

WELSHAMPTON

A495

N

To
Ellesmere

Shorter Route

Canal

Bridge
53

Bridge 52

Mill
House

Colemere

Car
Park

Colemere

14

Mill House.

which time the farmer who owns the field on the opposite bank allowed people to walk along the side of his field.

The trees on the opposite side of the canal surround Colemere, one of a collection of lakes or meres in this part of Shropshire and a wildlife sanctuary. There is a circular walk around the lake as well as plenty of shorter routes. If you wish to visit it later with the car, drive back down the lane on which you return to Welshampton, and go over the canal to a car park a little further on (see my map). The map-board at the car park will show you where the footpaths are.

At bridge 53, known as Mill Bridge, turn right up a short flight of wooden steps to the lane and turn right. Mill House is behind you, the other side of the bridge, and just beyond that is access to the circular path which goes right round the lake.

Walk up the lane away from the canal. At the crossroads go straight ahead into the lane with the sign 'Unsuitable for Motors'. At the main road, the A495, turn right for a short walk back to the village. For a little way there is no footpath, so take great care.

15

3 Market Drayton
The Four Alls

Ranking as one of the finest public houses in north-east
Shropshire is the Four Alls. Standing at a crossroads on the
A529, it is considerably enlarged from its original form, as the
photograph on the bar wall testifies. It was built as a farmhouse
around 1780 and it commenced commercial trading to supply
the needs of the bargees on the nearby canal. It is reputed to be
haunted though little is known of the ghost. The name dates
from an 18th-century joke and the original inn sign can be seen
on the bar wall. The sign outside is more recent but equally
conveys the reasoning behind the unusual name. There are four
people depicted on the sign: The King – I rule all, The Soldier
– I fight for all, The Bishop – I pray for all, and the luckless
citizen – I pay for all!

Families are very welcome in the comfortable and spacious
dining areas, of which there are many, and tables are set out on
the edge of the car park for those sunny days. The menu is
chalked up on a vast blackboard over the entire length of the

bar. I counted no less than 47 different dishes, not including the children's menu and the 'Chef's Daily Specials'. This vast array of food includes a roast of the day, cottage pie, lasagne, chicken chasseur, Texas beef, garlic scallops, curries, bacon chop, lamb and beef steaks, roast beef and Yorkshire pudding, steak and kidney pie, savoury mince, mixed grills and fish – plaice, Dover sole and scampi. You will also find a good selection of sweets. Meals are served from 11 am to 2.30 pm and 6 pm to 10 pm on Monday to Friday, and all day on Saturday. On Sunday a carvery is available from 12 noon to 3 pm. Throughout the week there are breakfasts (from 7 am to 10 am) and afternoon teas, too. Flowers Best Bitter, Heineken and Guinness are on offer, as well as Murphy's, Wadworth 6X, Boddingtons Bitter, Whitbread Best Bitter, and Blackthorn and Autumn Gold ciders. The bar is open from 11 am to 11 pm on Monday to Saturday, and from 12 noon to 3 pm and 7 pm to 10.30 pm on Sunday. Bed and breakfast accommodation is also offered.

Telephone: 01630 652995.

How to get there: Market Drayton is signposted north-east of Shrewsbury on the A53 road. Some 4 miles beyond Hodnet, at a roundabout at Ternhill, turn right onto the A41 and follow this for 1½ miles. At the first crossroads, and with RAF Ternhill on your right, turn left into an unclassified road signed 'Sutton'. Turn right at the T-junction in Sutton and you come to the A529 road. Turn left and the Four Alls is 100 yards ahead.

Parking: There is a large car park at the inn.

Length of the walk: 2½ miles. Map: OS Landranger 127 Stafford, Telford and surrounding area (inn GR 684320).

This is a very pleasant and easy walk along quiet lanes or sandy tracks. There is lovely scenery to the west on the way out and a visit to a nature reserve. On the way back you have a good view of Salisbury Hill. The walk is pushchair friendly.

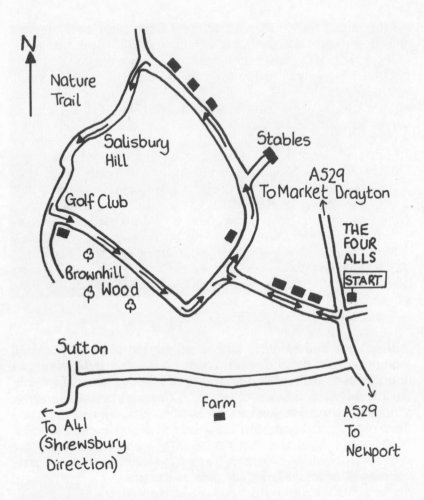

The Walk

From the pub, turn right past the original part of the building and right again down a narrow lane between hedges. The lane ends after ½ mile at a T-junction of tracks. Turn right along what is known locally as Sandy Lane and follow this past the elegant house on your left and over a slight rise. There is a good viewpoint near a small stables. Go straight ahead, through a facing gate and down the track. Passing Keepers Cottage and another house, come to a metalled lane and turn left.

A little way along this lane on your left is a Queen Victoria

The famous inn sign.

Jubilee seat and, directly opposite, the entrance to Walkmill nature reserve. An information board just inside tells you about it and what you may expect to see. If you wish to walk round, go to the right. The path eventually bends round to an iron bridge over the river and from here you take the track through the reeds, straight back to the gate.

Continue along the lane for ½ mile until you come to the Market Drayton golf course. Turn left and cross the car park, then pass the club house and join the sandy track just beyond it. As you walk along this track, look through the gap on your left to see Salisbury Hill. It was during the Wars of the Roses that Lord Salisbury was leading an army of 10,000 men from Ludlow to York. On arriving at Market Drayton he was confronted by a smaller number of Lancastrian troops and withdrew to what later became known as Salisbury Hill. In the ensuing battle it was Lord Salisbury who carried the day and triumphed at the battle of Blore Heath, about 5 miles to the north-east. Continue along the sandy track to the T-junction, where you rejoin the metalled lane and turn right to return to the Four Alls.

4 Llanyblodwel
The Horseshoe Inn

Situated in a hollow by a river, the inn must rank as one of the most picturesque of all pubs in Shropshire and, yes, it is in Shropshire despite the name conveying the contrary idea. It became anglicised in 1573. Before that, however, it was very much part of Wales and had been a Druid settlement as early as AD 200. Many battles were fought during the period of the Roman occupation, the hills around being rich in the copper, zinc and lead very much in demand in those times and, as you will see as you drive here or drive away, the scars of current quarrying still mark the hillsides. There has been a church here for 1,700 years and this is thought to be one of the oldest holy sites in Britain. The lychgate was erected in memory of William Henry Perry Leslie of Bryn Tanat, 2 miles south of Llanyblodwel, who chose *Jerusalem* as the anthem for the Women's Institute. The attractive packhorse bridge over the river Tanat dates from 1710.

The Horseshoe Inn is a most attractive building in typical

Shropshire black and white. Originally built as a farmhouse, the building dates from 1445 and its popularity is evidenced by the stream of customers pouring through its door. As it became a freehouse only in 1993 the new owners must be very satisfied with the results of their labours. Notice how the front of the building bulges, and see the mounting block, still in place. Inside is pure delight with thick oak beams and wall supports and in the corner of the bar the plaster has been removed to reveal the original infilling. Outside on the river side of the car park the row of picnic tables gives an ideal setting for lunch on a sunny summer day.

Marston's Pedigree, Foster's lager, John Smith's Bitter, Murphy's Irish Stout, Wrexham lager and Guinness are all on offer, alongside Dry Blackthorn cider. The large and varied menu includes scampi, fresh fish of the day, beef and ale pie, gammon, cottage pie, steaks, lasagne, chilli con carne and, at lunchtimes, freshly baked baguettes with various fillings. Starters and sweets are available and there is also a specials board. The opening hours are from 11 am to 11 pm on weekdays (sometimes closed between 3 pm and 6.30 pm at quiet times in the winter) and from 12 noon to 3 pm and 7 pm to 10.30 pm on Sunday.

Telephone: 01691 828969.

How to get there: Llanyblodwel is 5½ miles south-west of Oswestry, taking the A483 south then the A495. From Shrewsbury take the A5 Llangollen road and fork left after Nesscliffe, signposted 'B4396 Knockin', then continue to Llynclys. Go straight over at the junction with the A483 onto the A495, then, ignoring the 'Lake Vyrwny' sign, continue ahead, rejoining the B4396. After a further ¼ mile go straight ahead where the sign says 'Horseshoe Inn, Llanyblodwel'.

Parking: The inn has a large car park.

Length of the walk: 4 miles. Map: OS Landranger 126 Shrewsbury and surrounding area (inn GR 241228).

The walk is entirely by way of very quiet country lanes and is suitable for pushchairs. If you meet even one vehicle on this route it will be one more

21

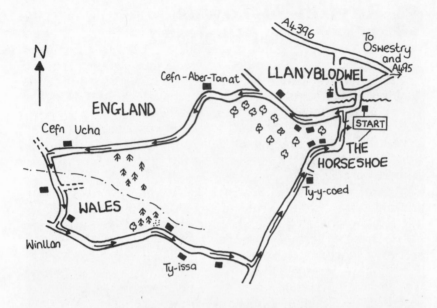

than is usually met! Once you get away to the area south-west of the A5 it is almost as if you take a step back in time. Here the lanes seem to lead nowhere in particular and are in no hurry to get there anyway! The walk begins in the valley and climbs gradually onto higher ground from where the views are really something.

The Walk

From the pub door, turn left and go straight ahead on a narrow lane which at first is level. At the fork of lanes, go uphill past Cefn-Aber-Tanat. Follow the lane on to Cefn Ucha where, turning left, you cross the border into Wales and drop down, then up a short, steep hill. At the T-junction turn left and continue along the lane, which goes downhill now, passing a forest entrance on the left at the bottom of the hill. After the next farm, Ty-issa, on the right, the lane rises again. Turn left at the next road junction and follow that lane over the hill and back down to Llanyblodwel. The views from up here are superb, with rolling hills stretching away into the distance, uncluttered and unspoilt by any kind of development. The air is sharp and clear and there is a peacefulness very difficult to find anywhere else.

22

5 Ruyton-XI-Towns
The Admiral Benbow

Your first reaction will be, that's an odd name, Ruyton-XI-Towns! To be truthful it is really Ruyton of the XI Towns. As a town it is very small, but as a village it is a reasonable size. However, it is a town and was once a borough in its own right. Ruyton is mentioned in the Domesday Book and the unusual appellation emanates from the eleven townships round about, which are, Ruyton, Coton, Shotatton, Shelvock, Eardiston, Wykey, West Felton, Haughton, Rednal, Sutton and Tedsmore.

Known locally as 'The Top House', the Admiral Benbow is a large 18th-century building opposite the church. Built around 1780 as a private dwelling, it still has the appearance as such. The inn gets its name from John Benbow, who was born in Shrewsbury in 1653 and rose to be a Vice-Admiral under King William III. A loyal and famous man of his day, Benbow's exploits against the French made him a popular hero. The lounge and public bars have open fires in season. Both bars are compact and comfortable and there is a separate family room.

Facilities for children include a high chair, pushchair, toys, books and changing facilities for babies. The garden at the back has tables and swings and, as an added interest for youngsters, geese, hens and ducks. There is an outside balcony. A wide range of beers are on offer, including Marston's and Banks's, as well as Murphy's Irish Stout, Stella Artois and Heineken lagers, and Strongbow and Woodpecker ciders. The menu is almost limitless and offers home-battered cod, chicken, scampi, curries, jacket potatoes and several hot-pots. The children's menu lists assorted burgers and sausages, and there are various vegetarian dishes. The pub is open from 11 am to 3 pm and 7 pm to 11 pm on weekdays, and all day on Saturday – when arrangements can be made for food out of usual meal hours, perhaps after your walk. On Sunday the times are 12 noon to 3 pm and 7 pm to 10.30 pm. Parties are asked to book in advance.

Telephone: 01939 260793.

How to get there: Ruyton-XI-Towns is north-west of Shrewsbury. Take the A5 trunk road towards Oswestry. Go through Nesscliffe and pass the road junction to Knockin. Just over a mile further, watch for the road junction 'T'-sign, the junction is just over the brow of an awkward rise with a bend on it. Turn right, signposted 'Ruyton-XI-Towns'.

Parking: Outside the front of the inn.

Length of the walk: 2 miles. Map: OS Landranger 126 Shrewsbury and surrounding area (inn GR 395221).

An easy stroll with some fine views. Mostly on quiet lanes with just one stretch of a grassy track, the walk is right away from the madding crowd. The route is level, with no gradients to speak of, and so is very pushchair friendly.

The Walk
From the inn cross the road and walk up the slope to the church. Built by the Normans around 1120, this is well worth a visit. In the churchyard, just to the left of the porch, the remains can be seen of the Norman castle built in 1155 and demolished by the Welsh in 1403. What an ideal site for a castle,

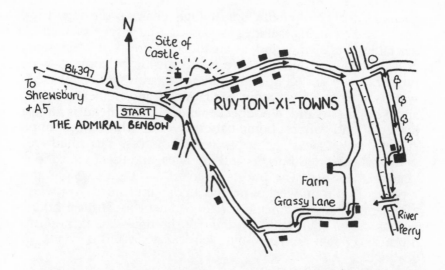

perched here on the high ground above the river. Walk round the church to the far side and you will see what I mean, for the castle was situated high above the surrounding land. The unusual war memorial is a cave hewn out of the red-sandstone rock on which the village stands. This stone is much in evidence in the construction of walls and houses and in Platt Bridge over the river Perry.

Leave the church by the lychgate and turn left along Church Street. A name which will be familiar to all is that of Sir Arthur Conan Doyle, the writer and creator of Sherlock Holmes. He lived in Ruyton for a short period in 1878, not as a writer but in his original calling, that of a physician. He was taken on as assistant by the local GP Dr Elliot, but stayed only four months in the post. At the bridge, when it is safe to do so, cross the road into Mill Lane and walk along this to Mill House, ignoring the one and only side turn to the right.

If you don't have a pushchair, the more interesting walk is to cross the bridge, pass the former tollhouse on the left, and then turn first right. Follow the track alongside the wood and when you get to the sewage works turn right around the outer fence and into a wide, grassy field, with the river on your right. The Perry is very attractive here with its flowering reeds and usually some ducks. When you reach the iron bridge, a good step up

A toll house along the route.

and down each end, cross it and the field beyond, to reach the lane and turn left to Mill House.

The metalled lane ends at Mill House, where a grassy track takes over. Passing the mill, the track turns to the right, later swinging left and then right again, giving, along this stretch, some superb views. The first after the left bend is east across rolling fields to The Wrekin, and the second, after the track swings right again, south to Caradoc, the pointed hill on the left, the Longmynd, which from here looks quite inconspicuous as a wide, flat hill, while to the right are the Stiperstones. Just before reaching the lane is a third viewpoint, south-west to the Breidden Hills, on top of which you may be able to see the Rodney monument.

On reaching the lane turn right. You arrive back in Ruyton by Little Ness Road. Continue ahead until you see Bay Cottage on your right and a small '30' sign. Go left here down a concrete ramp with a hand-rail in the middle, into Gooseberry Lane, and in a few yards you will be back at the inn.

6 Harmer Hill
The Bridgewater Arms

Harmer Hill is one of several rocky red-sandstone outcrops in the north Shropshire Plain. Others nearby are Pim Hill, which you pass on the way to Harmer Hill from Shrewsbury, and away to the east you can, on the walk, see Grinshill, while nearer to Shrewsbury and not visible from the walk is Haughmond Hill. These hills are the result of weathering whereby the stronger sandstone, being more resistant to the elements, has been left in a series of 'islands' surrounded by less durable land.

The Bridgewater Arms became a licensed premises around 1820, when the then owner was the Earl Brownlow. There was stabling for eight horses, which suggests a hostelry of good proportions and a significant flow of clientele. A large red-sandstone building, recently extended, the pub is situated on the left-hand side of the main road as you travel north, just at the fork where the roads to Wem and Ellesmere part company. Inside, the lounges and bars are spacious and extremely comfortable. There is a separate family dining-room, as well as a bar, a main eating section, and an outside play area for children. The menu runs to over 40 items, not including the specials board, and vegetarians are well catered for, as are children. The main menu has a variety of starters and the main courses include steak and kidney pie, Teviotdale pie, gammon, steak, chicken, steak and mushroom pudding, sweet 'n' sour chicken, scampi, plaice, fish pie. There are also salads and sandwiches. On Sunday a traditional roast is served. Heineken, Whitbread Trophy Bitter, Stella Artois, Murphy's Irish Stout, Whitbread Best Mild, Boddingtons Bitter, Morland Old Speckled Hen, Strong Pale Ale and Guinness are all on offer, along with Strongbow cider and two white wines. The opening hours on Monday to Saturday are from 11 am to 11 pm, and on Sunday from 12 noon to 10.30 pm, and meals are served all day from 11.30 am (12 noon on Sunday) until 10 pm.

Telephone: 01939 290377.

How to get there: Harmer Hill lies 7 miles north of Shrewsbury on the A528 Ellesmere road. From Shrewsbury leave by Coton Hill, the road alongside the river Severn, heading north to Harmer Hill. The pub stands at the junction of the A528 and the B5476 road to Wem.

Parking: There is a large car park at the pub.

Length of the walk: 3 miles. Map: OS Landranger 126 Shrewsbury and surrounding area (inn GR 490220).

The first part of this walk is through very pleasant pine woods, which are a feature of all the hills mentioned above. On emerging from the trees the walk crosses open fields with good views, to return along a little-used country lane.

The Walk
Leave the pub and turn left on the footpath alongside the main road. Shortly after passing the Red Castle inn, fork left downhill, as signposted 'Webscott', and follow a twisting lane called Lower Road, past the houses and towards the pine woods which deck the hill beyond. Opposite Moss Farm, turn right uphill, by the public footpath signpost, passing another red-

28

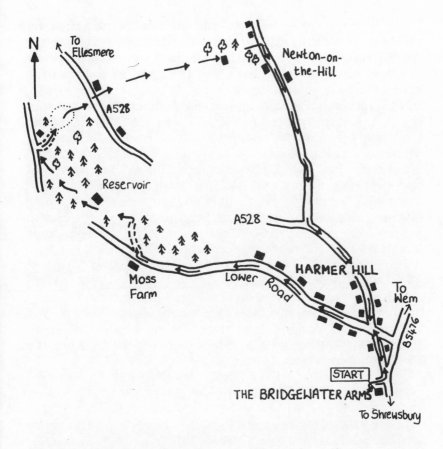

sandstone cottage, and continue on this track until you come to an open field. Turn left to the stile. Go straight across the field towards the grass-domed reservoir on the other side. There is a waymarked stile to the left of the reservoir and a footpath alongside it. If, however, the stile at the far end is unusable keep to the right of the reservoir on the edge of the field – there is ample room without treading on any crops.

On reaching the grit track, which is an access road for the reservoir, walk along it, with the fence on your left, until you come to a stile just after the right-hand bend. Turn left over the stile and follow a well-defined path through the pine trees. This then drops downhill gently to emerge again on Lower Road. Do not, however, go as far as the road. Passing on your right the

29

An unusual house built into the hillside.

barrier entrance to a disused quarry, turn right onto a sandstone track which goes alongside a cottage. As a guide look for the yellow danger sign on the wooden electricity pylon to the right of this track. Follow the track through the old quarry until it bends around to the right and by a flight of concrete steps rises to a waymarked gate at the top. Cross the fields straight ahead, as directed by the waymark arrow, to the main road, the A528. Go over the road to the public footpath sign on the other side and continue straight ahead across the middle of a wide field towards a small group of trees in the middle. Bear slightly right at the trees, where there is a two-armed footpath sign, and head for the hedge, beyond which there is a singular tubular iron gate at a corner in the hedgerow. In the new field go straight ahead, with the hedge on your left, towards the distant farm buildings.

At the next gate, with a line of trees on the left which are used as a pheasant rearing area, a cover to give it its proper name, go ahead over the stile, still keeping by the fence on your left, and in the top left-hand corner is a stile which enables you to cross the cover to the lane beyond. I learned from the farmer something of the history of this path. The two buildings on your left as you reach the lane were, in order of appearance, once the minister's manse and a chapel. Having no burial ground of their own, coffins were taken from the chapel by the mourners to Myddle churchyard for burial, thus creating the path by which you arrived. All the public footpaths had some original utilitarian purpose, other than pleasure for which they are used today, and this path is no exception. It also appears that in the 18th century this area had many more residents than there now are, and in the last field the farmer had found remains from several houses which once stood there. On reaching the lane, turn right and follow it all the way back to the A528 road. Turn left onto the pavement and the village sign for Harmer Hill is only a few yards further on. Continue along the road back to the start.

7 Shrewsbury
The Red Barn

The Red Barn in Longden Road is a mock-Tudor building built during the 1920s. Extremely comfortable inside, it has a splendid south-facing sun lounge. Outside there is a sizable area where children can play in perfect safety, as well as a garden area with tables. Being modern, the pub lacks the time-worn atmosphere associated with older buildings but this is more than compensated for by the spacious interior and excellent food. The menu caters for all tastes. A wide variety of starters can be followed by, for example, steak, plaice, scampi, garlic and herb chicken, gammon steak, mixed grill, chicken tikka masala, prawns Cantonese or lamb with Stilton dumplings. In addition, you will find a daily specials board, a vegetarian menu and children's portions. Sunday lunch is a traditional roast. Greenalls Original and Mild, Tennent's Extra, Guinness, Carling Black Label, Labatt's and Tetley Bitter are on offer, alongside Strongbow and Woodpecker ciders. The opening hours are from 11 am to 3 pm and 6 pm to 11 pm on weekdays, and

12 noon to 3 pm and 7 pm to 10.30 pm on Sunday. Telephone: 01743 362503.

How to get there: Longden Road is on the south side of Shrewsbury. From the town leave by Wyle Cop and the English Bridge. Pass under the railway bridge, follow the one-way traffic system round to the right, under the railway arches, and then bear left signed Belle Vue. At the next road junction, just a few yards on, turn right. This is Longden Road.

Parking: There is a large car park at the pub.

Length of the walk: 2½ miles. Map: OS Landranger 126 Shrewsbury and surrounding area (inn GR 488114).

I have designed this walk to bring in all the major attractions of Shrewsbury. The first part of the walk traverses the residential area of Kingsland with its elegant houses and spacious grounds, then, crossing the river, you come to the earlier town houses of Swan Hill and Belmont, before reaching the oldest parts of the town around Bear Steps. Most of Shrewsbury's finest buildings will be passed along this walk, which I hope will encourage you to take a guided walk another day.

The Walk
Turn right out of the car park and walk a few yards to a bungalow on the right, Pathways, alongside which is a narrow tarmac path with the sign 'cycling prohibited' on it. Turn right and follow the path downhill and across Rea Brook. At the junction of paths up the slope, continue ahead.

This part of Shrewsbury contains large houses of very distinctive architecture, many of which now form part of Shrewsbury School. Cross over the road into Greville Road, at the end of which turn right into Ashton Road. The fine ornate entrance gates to Shrewsbury School are on the left. Continue ahead at the next junction, past the sign 'Access restricted 150 yards ahead'. Turn left at the railings into a narrow path, which may be muddy at times, to emerge onto the grassy slopes overlooking Shrewsbury.

'High the vanes of Shrewsbury gleam
Islanded in Severn stream;

The bridges from the steepled crest
Cross the water east and west.'

So wrote A.E. Housman in his book of verse *A Shropshire Lad* and from this viewpoint you can easily see the sight which inspired these immortal lines. With the public front of Shrewsbury School behind you look out over the river to the Quarry, the town's park, dominated beyond by St Chad's church.

Follow the path past the school chapel, the second building on your left and, just before a stile, turn right downhill between chestnut trees. When you get to the bottom, by the boathouse, turn left along the riverside path. This passes in front of a second boathouse where you will find the first of three information boards – this one tells you about the Quarry. Nearing the Chain Bridge, bear right to a kissing-gate and then turn right to cross the bridge.

On reaching the far bank, turn right and walk along one of the many lime tree walks that are such a feature of the Quarry. Turn left by the statue of Hercules, near which is a second information board, this time about the wildlife on the river, and walk towards St Chad's church, built in the late 1790s. The enclosed area on the right, halfway along, contains the formal garden area of the park, always a feature, and a good midway stopping place with many seats. Reaching the main gate and the attractive war memorial, cross the road, Town Walls, to enter St Chad's churchyard, now landscaped as a woodland garden. The entrance is just round to the left. One tomb of note is that of Ebenezer Scrooge. After a film was made here in 1985 the film company left the tombstone in place. Follow the path ahead to the main path and turn left and it is on the left.

Leave the churchyard by the other gate and cross the road again, turning left along Town Walls. This was, in ancient times, the south side of the town walls and a gatehouse still remains. Turn left into St John's Hill and continue ahead into the town. Pass the new Market Hall on the left and turn right into Princess Street to find the Square, one of Shrewsbury's main attractions. The tourist information centre (telephone: 01743 350761) is on your right. The old Market Hall dates from 1596 and dominates the Square.

Cross the Square to the left, passing the Market Hall and

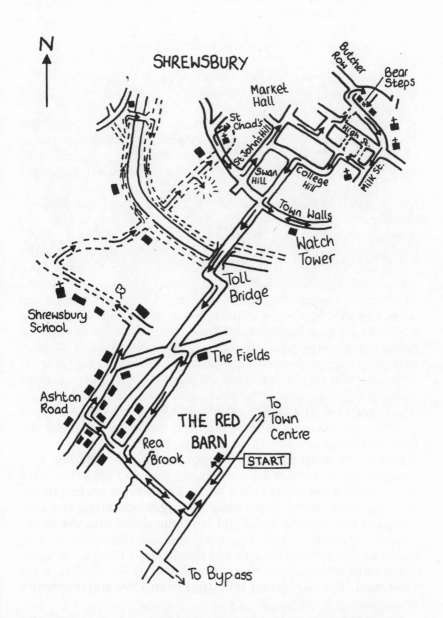

N

SHREWSBURY

Butcher Row
Bear Steps
Market Hall
St Chad's
St John's Hill
High St.
Swan Hill
College Hill
Milk St.
Town Walls
Watch Tower
Toll Bridge
Shrewsbury School
The Fields
Ashton Road
To Town Centre
THE RED BARN
Rea Brook
START
To Bypass

Shrewsbury and the river Severn.

beyond it the statue of Lord Clive of India. Turn right into High Street but immediately cross the road towards Jones the Outfitters and enter Grope Lane, one of the many narrow streets of old Shrewsbury, with houses jutting out on either side. At the top of Grope Lane turn left along a cobbled street and go round the corner to the Prince Rupert Hotel. Look left down Butchers Row, another of Shrewsbury's fine old streets. Turn right now into St Alkmund's Place and right again by Powney's bookshop.

In front of you is Shrewsbury's most distinguished landmark, Bear Steps. Complete renovation has taken place and the building is now much as it would have been 500 years ago. It houses the offices of all the leading conservation bodies of the town and county. The plaque on the wall tells you more about it. Descend the steps and turn left along Fish Street. Cross High Street again into Milk Street. The Old Post Office Hotel on the left is another building of note – you may observe the old fire insurance badge on the front wall above the shop front. Turn right into Princess Street and here you pass two 'shutts', the local name for a passage. The first is the Golden Cross Passage with the inn sign above it (note the plaque on the wall which tells you more about it) and the second is Peacock Passage, opposite which you turn left up College Hill.

On the building at the corner of College Hill, with the sign 'No 1 College Hill' prominently displayed you can just make out the words 'County Savings Bank'. A little further along College Hill, down a passage to the left, is the Clive House Museum. Continue towards the Admiral Benbow public house and turn left into Swan Hill. Notice the carving in the stonework over the office windows opposite. Turn left at the end of Swan Hill, rejoining Town Walls. The leaning tower ahead, now in the care of the National Trust, is the sole remaining medieval guard tower of the old town walls. Opposite this are the entrance gates to Swan Hill Court House, an elegant country mansion built in the days when land was not at a premium in the town, for the Marquis of Bath. It dates from 1761.

Continue past the tower and the elegant crescent to a good viewpoint from the Town Walls. Then return past the tower to the Kingsland Road and turn left to cross the toll bridge (fee 1p).

At the end of Kingsland Road, cross the road junction diagonally to what at first appears to be the drive to the house called The Fields, but here you bear right into Beehive Lane and, following that, rejoin the outward walk just above the bridge across Rea Brook, and so retrace your steps back to the Red Barn.

8 Hanwood
The Cock Inn

Although just a quiet country village today, Hanwood has been, in its time, quite industrious. During the 19th century the population of just six families in 1086 grew to around 300 people. The 18th-century paper mill became a flax, yarn and thread finishing factory by 1820 and many cottages were built to house the work force. Later cotton took over until the company closed in 1886. The mill continued until 1922, grinding ore. Another product of the area was coal, which was mined within a 2½ mile radius of the village, and various spoil tips are identified on the map outside the pub.

The Cock Inn stands between the road and the Cambrian Railway. The inn was built on this present site in 1860 when the original building, situated at the Shrewsbury end of the village, was demolished to make way for the railway. It has a splendid garden for children, with swings, climbing nets and many other amusements, plus a small collection of rabbits and an aviary. The lounge bar is spacious and comfortably furnished. Carling

Black Label, Tennent's Extra, Greenalls Mild and Bitter and Tetley Bitter are all on offer, as well as Guinness and Strongbow cider. The extensive menu includes steaks, chicken, gammon, chicken Kiev, plaice and cod, lasagne, vegetarian dishes, ploughman's lunches and sandwiches. You will also find a children's menu and a daily specials board. A traditional roast is served on Sunday. The pub is open from 11.30 am to 3 pm and 7 pm to 11 pm on Monday to Friday (no meals on Monday evening) and all day, 11.30 am to 11 pm, on Saturday. The usual Sunday hours, 12 noon to 3 pm and 7 pm to 10.30 pm, apply.
Telephone: 01743 860392.

How to get there: Hanwood is 4 miles south-west of Shrewsbury on the A488 Pontesbury/Bishop's Castle road.

Parking: There are two car parks at the pub.

Length of the walk: 2½ miles. Map: OS Landranger 126 Shrewsbury and surrounding area (inn GR 443097)

There is a map plaque on the wall of the Cock Inn, just outside the front door, showing all the footpaths around Hanwood. The walk I describe goes via Orchard Lane to Coppice Farm, then past Wood Hall to Moat Hall and back, making a large, rather out-of-shape square! There are some nice views and the walking is easy on the whole though a very short stretch near Moat Hall can be wet at times so boots are advisable.

The Walk
From the pub, cross the road and turn right. After going over the Rea Brook cross in front of Hanwood village stores to the garage and bear slightly left into Orchard Lane. This ends in a grassy stretch between two hedges. Cross the stile and continue ahead up the field, with a fence on your left. Across to your right you can see the Breidden Hills and the keen eyed will be able to make out Rodney's Pillar on the top.
In the top left-hand corner of the field, by the trees, cross the stile and follow a narrow, grassy path past two houses on either side before reaching the metalled lane. Turn left. Passing Coppice Farm on your left, continue to Wood Hall, an impressive three-storey brick building set back from the lane.

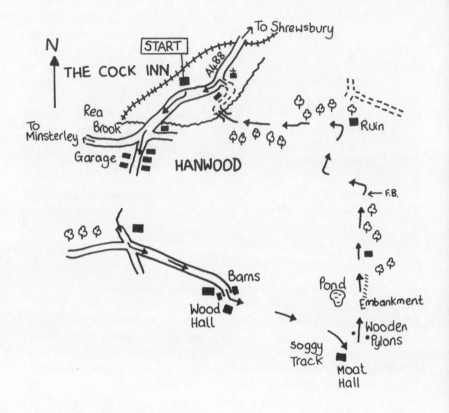

Go straight ahead between the farm outbuildings and then bear left to a field gate. A grassy track beyond the gate goes to Moat Hall. Walk along the edge of the field, with the hedge on your left. After the next stile the track can be rather waterlogged after wet weather, so walk along the edge of the field, and at the end of this field return to the track which bears to the right, to reach Moat Hall. Pass through a gap in a fence to arrive at Moat Hall. Go as far as the field gate, where you will find a two-armed footpath sign. Turn hard left and follow the well-defined track, which passes under overhead electricity wires and alongside a fence on your left. Go through a facing gate, passing close to the pond and continuing ahead, with a hedge on your left, on a causeway above the fields. Go through a second waymarked gate

An attractive farmhouse along the route.

and straight on at the barn ahead, ignoring the well-defined track which swings to the right. Keep the trees on your right now and this area is shown, on the map outside the pub, as a 'Pit Mound'.

When the trees end cross an almost unseen bridge and turn left to the field gate. Go ahead now around two sides of the field, keeping the hedge on your left. At the second corner you will find a gate flanked by three waymarks. Following the yellow arrow, go through the gate and straight on. Don't go towards the more easily noticeable gate, but head across the field, keeping the Breidden Hills dead ahead. There is a waymarked stile midway between two oak trees. Go over the stile and bear slightly left across the last field, still heading directly towards the Breidden Hills, which are now slowly disappearing behind the tops of the trees.

As the trees close in at the corner of the field you will find a gully joining from your left. Follow this for a few yards to your right and there is a gate and a stile. Cross the grassy area beyond and a white-painted footbridge and, skirting the backs of several gardens, come back into Hanwood by Church Lane. As you turn left at the road the Cock Inn is now in sight.

9 Pontesbury
The Red Lion

The parish church of St George is close to the Red Lion and well worth a visit – it is a most impressive building dating from the 12th century. Part of Pontesford Hill, around which you walk, is called Earl's Hill and was developed as a nature reserve by a resident in the village. It is now in the ownership of the Shropshire Wildlife Trust.

Right in the centre of Pontesbury and bedecked with baskets of flowers throughout the summer is the Red Lion. Originally a stable, it became an inn around 1750 and was known then as the Angel. It isn't recorded when or why the name changed but even Red Lion is a misnomer as, according to the deeds, it should be just the Lion. Families are very welcome and can use either the lounge bar or the dining-room. During the summer tables are set out at the side of the inn. The menu includes plaice and scampi, steaks, chicken and lighter meals such as

ploughman's lunches, also starters and sweets. Vegetarian food is available, as well as children's portions. Guinness, Tetley, Greenall Mild and Bitter and Strongbow cider are all on offer. The opening hours are from 11 am to 3 pm and 6.30 pm to 11 pm on Monday to Saturday, with the usual Sunday hours, 12 noon to 3 pm and 7 pm to 10.30 pm.
Telephone: 01743 7970321.

How to get there: Pontesbury is south-west of Shrewsbury on the A488 road to Bishop's Castle. The inn is facing you as you come into the centre of the village.

Parking: At the pub but space is limited. The landlord will direct you to alternative parking close by.

Length of the walk: 2½ or 3¼ miles. Map: OS Landranger 126 Shrewsbury and surrounding area (inn GR 400060).

Pontesford Hill, which merges with Earl's Hill, is reminiscent of a crouching lion when viewed from afar. This is an undulating walk which circles the hill and, by keeping on the lower slopes, the walking is reasonably easy with no steep climbs.

The Walk
From the pub cross the road towards the shops and turn right into Chapel Street. Pass the chapel and turn left at the Plough Inn. Turn left at The Grove by the letterbox and walk up the lane towards the hill. Go straight on at the road junction where there is a 'No Through Road' sign. The metalled road peters out and becomes a track.
For the shorter walk, turn left at the T-junction of tracks and go through the gate by the Shropshire Wildlife Trust notice board. Walk up the grassy track for 20 yards and find an inconspicuous stile in the fence on the left. Go over that and you soon join a wide, flat and easy to follow track which takes you along the west side of the hill to rejoin the lane (see below).
For the main walk, continue ahead on the level on a flat, wide track, bridged overhead by trees (there is a partly concealed bridleway sign on the corner). Go straight on through the gate, following the blue arrow. The track peters out in the field. Carry

43

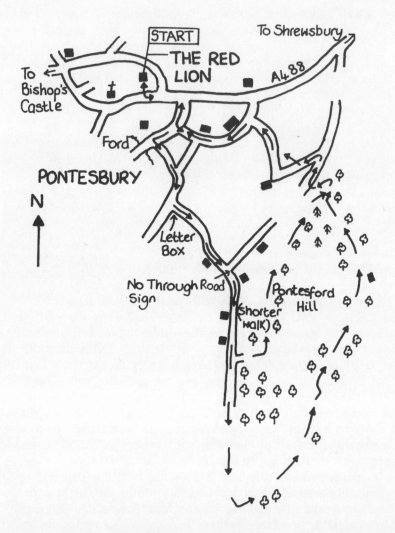

straight on, with the hedge on the left, through the first field gate. Cross the second field, with the hedge on the right, to the second gate by a waymark post sprouting yellow and blue waymark signs! Go through the gate and turn left along a grassy track and, going through the waymarked field gate in front, follow the direction of the blue arrow straight ahead, with the hedge to your left. A narrow track made by the farm animals will

18th century labourers' cottages at Pontesbury.

soon be found and you follow this, past the end of the hedge, where you bear slightly uphill to a stile now visible near the far left-hand corner of the field. Cross the stile and at the waymark post just beyond, turn right along the hillside path. The path now is straight ahead, clearly defined and waymarked. At the gate leading out of the area protected by the Shropshire Wildlife Trust you will find an information board. Go straight on across the field to rejoin the well-defined track beyond and in about ten minutes you come to the lane (the short route rejoins here).

Turn right down the hill and at the bottom turn left by a public footpath sign (arm missing) and cross the cattle grid. Go over the next cattle grid by a house and fork right, diagonally, across a field, heading towards the school, to a stile visible in the far corner. (If you have a pushchair, keep to the track towards the farm and turn right there.) On reaching the track turn right.

At the lane by the school turn left and follow the lane until, having passed the school and the cemetery, you turn right at the next road junction into Chapel Street again and the Red Lion.

10 **Pulverbatch**
The White Horse

A rhyme written by a local in 1770 augurs well for a visit to the White Horse:

> 'Cothercott upon the hill
> Wilderley down in the dale
> Churton for pretty girls
> and Pulverbatch for good ale.'

In addition to Pulverbatch, or Castle Pulverbatch to give it its full name, we pass two of the other three places mentioned here on this walk and view the third from a distance.

Ever since I moved to this part of Shropshire in 1960, the White Horse has ranked highly in my esteem for the quality of its food. It is a most impressive place. You have only to step out of your car to be aware of the mouth-watering smell emanating from the kitchens of this 13th-century coaching inn. The Rob Roy lounge is cosy and comfortable, with a wealth of oak beams and oak supports and decked with Highland paintings. An open fire is welcoming during the colder weather, in the oldest part of the lounge. I can recall the days when the front door was at the front and the upper lounge was for restaurant purposes only. Now the pub's popularity has demanded more room and it all forms an integral whole, with the addition of a recently-converted extra lounge and bar on busy days. The former front door area is now a cosy little snug, just right for a small family. The licensees hail from Scotland, which accounts for the distinct Scottish flavour in the decor and many items on the menu!

The menu offers choices to satisfy every possible taste, but I go there for the chicken, basted in the pub's own home-made breadcrumb batter – I have never tasted anything like it anywhere else! The portions are ample and there is a wide range of starters and main courses, including gammon, pork, scampi, sole, chicken chasseur, beef Stroganoff and Scotch trout, as well as a variety of uniquely Scottish dishes. You will find vegetarian food and a children's menu, lighter snacks such as sandwiches, burgers, salads, jacket potatoes and omelettes, two specials blackboards and sweets. Meals are served from 12 noon to 1.40 pm and 7 pm to 10 pm. Heineken, Murphy's Irish Stout, Flowers Original, Wadworth 6X, Boddingtons Bitter, Stella Artois and Guinness are among the beers and there is Strongbow cider. The opening hours are from 12 noon to 3 pm (2 pm on Sunday) and 7 pm to 11 pm (10 pm on Sunday).

Telephone: 01743 718247.

How to get there: Pulverbatch is 9 miles south-west of Shrewsbury. Take the unclassified Longden road which is roughly halfway between the A488 Bishop's Castle road and the A49 trunk road to Ludlow. It is signposted 'Longden' and 'Nuffield Hospital' from the B4380 – this road cannot be accessed from the A5 bypass. Continue to Pulverbatch. The pub is on the right at the end of the village.

Parking: There is a large car park behind the pub.

Length of the walk: 3 miles. Map: OS Landranger 126 Shrewsbury and surrounding area (inn GR 425025).

A gentle walk through attractive countryside, along quiet back lanes and using part of the Shropshire Way, a circular country walk. The castle site at Castle Pulverbatch can be seen from the walk and explored later, while along the way we pass the less distinct remains of a motte and bailey at Wilderley.

The Walk
Turn left out of the pub and walk through the village. At the end of the village fork right onto a narrow lane, signposted 'Church Pulverbatch', and follow it to the next village, about ½ mile. This village is also known locally as Churton so that makes up the second of the four places mentioned in the rhyme. The church has a circular churchyard and has been a religious site since the 13th century. At the triangular green in the centre of the village, opposite the church, fork right onto a wide, grassy track with hedges on both sides. Follow this for another ½ mile. At the next lane, bear left and walk along it until you come to Wilderley, the third of the places in the rhyme. Pass the farm, or Wilderley Hall as it is marked on the Ordnance Survey map, on the right and then turn right along a grassy track, marked with the Shropshire Way sign on the footpath signpost. The site of the motte and bailey castle is between the first and second field gates on the right. It's covered with trees now and hardly noticeable.

The grassy track ends at a field gate, alongside which is a wicket gate and the Shropshire Way sign on the post. Continue straight ahead. The boggy area by the gate soon gives way to a wide, grassy field with the hedge on the left. At the next track, by Beeches Farm, a red-brick farmhouse on the left, turn right and walk along a rough but dry track to Sheppen Fields Farm where you join a metalled lane. During the Middle Ages, up to the time of the Dissolution of the Monasteries, the lands here formed part of the Haughmond Abbey Estate. Haughmond Abbey is situated just north of Shrewsbury on the road to Newport, and is now in the care of English Heritage. The age of the farm, though not, perhaps, the present building, can be gauged from the name as sheep were kept on the hills by the monks, hence the name Sheppen.

Pass the farm and follow the lane back to Pulverbatch. Through the gateways on the left you will be able to see Cothercott Hill, the fourth place in the rhyme. It's the nearest

48

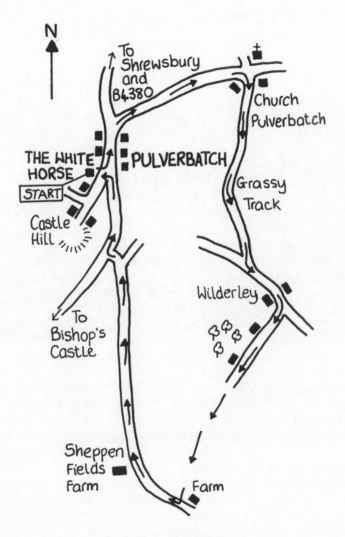

N

To
Shrewsbury
and
B4380

Church
Pulverbatch

THE WHITE
HORSE

PULVERBATCH

START

Grassy
Track

Castle
Hill

To
Bishop's
Castle

Wilderley

Sheppen
Fields
Farm

Farm

of the many hills and is shaped rather like an upturned pudding basin. Pass the first road junction and continue downhill toward a row of houses. The Pulverbatch castle mound is in front and slightly to the left as you reach the junction of roads. It can be accessed from the lane which goes uphill from the front of the White Horse. Turn right at the next road junction and, walking up a slight rise, return to the pub.

⑪ Ironbridge
Ye Olde Robin Hood

Built on high ground overlooking the river Severn in the 17th century, Ye Olde Robin Hood has been a public house since 1828, apart from a brief period between 1969 and 1975 when it was an antique shop. There was once stabling for two horses here. From its prominent position the inn looks over the river and the new Free Bridge, completed in 1994, replacing an earlier single line bridge. In 1871 the licensee Mr D. Boden was fined 5/- plus 11/- costs for being open outside licensing hours.

The inn has a spacious and very comfortable lounge with several side nooks. It is rich in unspoilt oak beams and has a pleasant, restful atmosphere. The food is superb and there are large helpings of it! Outside there is an attractive sun terrace with tables. Tennent's Extra, Highgate Dark Ale, Bass, Brew XI, Worthington Best Bitter, Guinness, and Carling Black Label and Tennent's Pilsner lagers are all on offer, alongside Woodpecker and Strongbow ciders. The menu includes various ploughman's lunches, burgers, salads and soup, scampi, plaice, cod, trout,

pizza, chicken, shark steaks, salmon, meat lasagne, chilli con carne, macaroni cheese and home-made steak and kidney pie, to name but a few. There is a children's menu, as well as sweets. Lunches are available from 12 noon to 2 pm. The opening hours are from 11.30 am to 3 pm and 6.30 pm to 11 pm on weekdays, all day Saturday in the summer. On Sunday the pub is open from 12 noon to 3 pm and 7 pm to 10.30 pm.
Telephone: 01952 433100.

How to get there: Ironbridge is situated south-east of Shrewsbury, between Telford and Bridgnorth. From Shrewsbury take the A458 as far as Much Wenlock. Here, turn left, opposite the Gaskell Arms, onto the A4169, signed 'Buildwas Abbey'. Over the bridge at Buildwas, turn right for Ironbridge, on the B4373. Drive through Ironbridge and beyond the chemist's shop, fork right, signposted 'Broseley'. Ye Olde Robin Hood is on your left as you reach the junction with the Free Bridge, and the car park entrance is just beyond.

Parking: There is a large car park at the inn.

Length of the walk: 2 ½ miles. Map: OS Landranger 127 Stafford, Telford and surrounding area (inn GR 681033).

The walk passes at first through some delightful deciduous woods before arriving at the famous Blists Hill Museum. Blists Hill is the largest of the museums and the first to be opened. It covers 50 acres and is a step back in time to the Victorian era, even to the extent of using Victorian money. It is a fully working museum, complete with a pub, candle factory and a butcher making real pies. The brochure says to allow at least 2½ hours, but I think this is on the conservative side. The return walk passes close to the Coalport China Museum and several other museums on the other side of the river, ending with a short stretch of the former Severn Valley Railway track, now used as a footpath.

The Walk
From the car park take the steep path uphill at the side of the inn, alongside the wooden fence. At the top turn right along Wesley Road. Opposite a street lamp fixed to telephone post No 47710, fork left onto a rough track going uphill. Pass in front of

a cottage and, before the wicket gate into the garden, turn hard right onto an overgrown track alongside the fence (on your left). In just a few yards through the trees turn left up a short slope towards a wooden electricity pylon and there you will find that the path opens out into a wide clearing with patches of heather. Go straight ahead and, at the third pylon and in sight of the road below, turn left into woods and start climbing the flight of wooden steps. Ignoring a level path on the left halfway up, bear right to a second flight of steps and later bear left to a third and a fourth flight, which then brings you to a second clearing with patches of heather.

A notice-board telling you about coppicing will confirm you are on route. Bear right across the clearing to find a well-defined path in the far corner which soon skirts an overgrown pond choked with bulrushes. The path is now easy to follow with several short flights of steps here and there until eventually you come to a T-junction opposite a field. Turn left up a short hill where shortly you will pass two former charcoal kilns and examples of the original and finished products. A wide track now leads you out of the wood, passing former brick kilns (on the left), onto the main road. Turn left along the road for 200 yards. At the private car park opposite Hillcrest, bear half-right towards the far right-hand corner. A path drops gently down to join another path. Turn left into the tunnel. (If you wish to visit the Blists Hill museum turn right.) You are now walking along the Silkin Way, a former railway line.

After 15 minutes or so you come to the famous Great Hay Incline bridge. Continue a little further until you come to a unique signpost, the wheel of a railway locomotive, set in concrete. Now turn right down a flight of steps to a large car park and picnic area by the Shakespeare Inn. Cross the road to a wooden field gate nearly opposite with a nice grassy bank for picnics and rests. Bear right on a rough track which bends left to the canal then back right again to a café and the entrance to the Tar Tunnel. Go up some steps and turn left over the bridge (narrow road). This is the end of the canal and from the bridge there is a very good view of the Great Hay Incline, with its railway still in place, the subject of many a photograph and picture postcard. The incline was used to raise barges from the canal basin below to the next section of the canal at the top. The

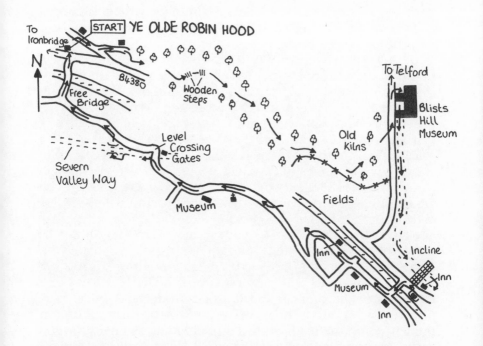

canal, opened in 1793 was mainly used for carrying coal from the various Shropshire coalfields to Blists Hill foundry and the Coalport china works. It started at Coalport, on the river Severn, and joined the Shrewsbury canal just north of Wellington, at Wappenshall. Now turn left, signed 'Severn Valley Way' and, dropping down the other side of the canal basin, cross the river by a footbridge. Note the plaques on the left denoting this bridge as a war memorial.

By the Boat Inn turn right along Ferry Road, which soon becomes a path behind the Jackfield Mill, Maws Craft Centre and Dancing Clows café. Cross straight over onto a tarmac path to reach the Half Moon Inn with its imitation black and white framework painted on a brick wall! Follow the approach road to a hair-pin bend, where you turn right by a short post, painted in red and white bands. A rough path now dips down to the river, then left up towards the church where you join a proper road. Continue ahead by Crossing Cottage, opposite the entrance to the Jackfield Tile Museum. A footpath, using the

The Ironbridge.

track bed of the former Shrewsbury – Bridgnorth railway begins just beyond the Chapel Lane street sign (note the original level crossing gates still in place). Walk along this, part of the Severn Valley Way, as far as the first footbridge, then turn left through a gap onto a tarmac road. Turn right now and walk under the former railway bridge to the road ahead. Turn left and the Free Bridge, with Ye Olde Robin Hood the other side, is just a few steps away.

12 All Stretton
The Yew Tree

Before the A49 bypass was built in the late 1930s the narrow winding road which runs through All Stretton was the main north-south route and the importance of the Yew Tree is easy to imagine. Built in 1720 as an alehouse, it still fulfils this function in a most satisfying manner! Sadly, the tree from which it gets its name was felled in 1980 but there are still two others in the gardens with several hundreds of years to go before they catch up with their fallen sister. The inn has a large garden and play area for children with outside tables, and the view adds greatly to the enjoyment of the meal. The lounge is large and very comfortable, with thick oak beams and horse brasses everywhere. The big open fireplace has a real fire during the cooler weather and the whole atmosphere is cosy and welcoming.

The menu caters for all tastes. After the starters, the list includes a choice of steaks, home-made steak and kidney pie, chicken curry, chilli con carne, plaice, cod and scampi, a range of basket meals, jacket potatoes, sandwiches and ploughman's lunches. There is a daily specials blackboard, from which the home-made venison pie, when available, is a house speciality. Vegetarian and children's menus are also available. Guinness, Carling Black Label, M&B Mild, Worthington Best Bitter, Bass, Caffrey's Irish Ale and Tennent's Extra are all on offer, as well as Dry Blackthorn and Autumn Gold ciders. Meals are served from 12 noon to 2 pm and 7 pm to 9 pm. On weekdays the Yew Tree is open from 11 am to 2.30 pm and 7 pm to 11 pm, and on Sunday from 12 noon to 3 pm and 7 pm to 10.30 pm.

Telephone: 01694 722228.

How to get there: From Shrewsbury drive south on the A49. After passing the Little Chef, fork right, signed 'Cardingmill Valley' and All Stretton is the first village you come to. The Yew Tree is on the right-hand side.

Parking: There is a large car park at the inn.

Length of the walk: 2½ miles. Map: OS Landranger 137, Ludlow, Wenlock Edge and surrounding area (inn GR 460954).

The Longmynd is the principal attraction of the Stretton area and the walk will act as an introduction to this very popular, but not overcrowded, area of wild upland. The views from the highest point of this route are excellent and take in a wide sweep of the north Shropshire Plain. By contrast the deep valley by which you return has its own charm, with a stream and much wildlife.

The Walk

From the pub, turn right and right again by the sign 'Village Hall', and walk up the lane. The half-timbered cottage behind the high hedge on the right is 17th century. The date 1683 is inscribed on the side facing the lane. Fork right up a wide track, which starts opposite the 'No Through Road' sign. The track climbs steadily before levelling out at another lane. Walk on up this lane, with occasional glimpses of the view north (to the right) and, after crossing the cattle grid, bear left along a flat, grassy track with a waymark post on it, inscribed 'High Park'. If you want to see the view, continue along the road a few yards towards Plush Hill, then return to the walk.

At the corner of the fence behind Plush Hill turn left at a second post marked with a blue bridleway arrow. Follow a wide, grassy track, which sweeps gently round to the right. You have a side arm of the valley on your left and a hillock on your right and, just ahead, a short bank. At the top of the bank turn left along another grassy, but indistinct track, with ferns on your left and wild grasses on your right. In the distance you can see the wide, green, grassy sward of Church Stretton golf links. There is no track now – it widens to become a grassy area. Bear gently to the right, keeping the valley to your left, but don't turn away from it. Eventually, you will come to more level ground, with a steep valley side to your left and still the area of wild grasses to your right. Continue near the edge of the valley slope to find a narrow, stony track which comes up the hillside at an oblique angle on your left. It ends by a small depression on your

A 17th century cottage in All Stretton.

right with a low rock face behind it. Ahead you can see the large rocky outcrop called Jonathan's Rock.

Turn sharp left now down this stony track, which zig-zags to the valley bottom by the stream. Turn left at the stream and walk down a wide, grassy path alongside it. Keep to the left of the stream until past the first holiday home. Soon cross the stream by a plank bridge and turn left by a cottage called The Batch. Walk on down the valley on a wide track, with the stream to your left, to return to the village. The area just before the cattle grid is a popular place with children and there is parking on the grass. This is the site of the former All Stretton reservoir, filled in during the 1960s. All the reservoirs in the hills, of which two remain, are now disused – a great pity.

13 Little Stretton
The Ragleth Inn

Little Stretton has four notable buildings, the church, the Manor House, the Ancient House, all half-timbered in traditional Shropshire style, and the Ragleth Inn.

Families are made very welcome and can use the main bar and the comfortable dining-room. There is also a large garden with tables, at the back, with access through the gate by the front door. Inside, the inn is cosy and welcoming, with oak-beamed ceilings and fires from autumn to spring. The menu includes plaice, scampi, various steaks and gammon, and you will find a daily specials board as well as a variety of sweets and vegetarian dishes. Foster's, Beamish, Stella, John Smith's Bitter, Marston's Pedigree and Strongbow cider are all served, and during the busy periods there are guest beers. An alternative to eating in is offered in the form of hot take-away pies. On Monday to Saturday the inn is open from 12 noon to 2.30 pm and 6 pm to 11 pm, and on Sunday from 12 noon to 3 pm and 7 pm to 10.30 pm. Bed and breakfast accommodation is available.

Telephone: 01694 722711.

How to get there: Little Stretton is situated 1 mile south of Church Stretton on the B4370, which runs parallel to the A49 Shrewsbury to Ludlow road. The inn is in the centre of the village, close to the famous half-timbered church.

Parking: There is a large car park at the inn.

Length of the walk: 3 miles. Map: OS Landranger 137, Ludlow, Wenlock Edge and surrounding area (inn GR 445919).

This is a superb walk. Once across the A49 at Little Stretton, you will find every footpath signposted and waymarked and every stile in immaculate order. The walk is undulating, with an uphill trend on the outward leg as far as The Hough. There are several stiles on the walk and a few flimsy nettles in the wood on the way back so young limbs will need protection. This walk is not really suitable for pushchairs.

The Walk

From the Ragleth car park, turn right and follow the road south, passing on your left the attractive half-timbered church and the Manor House. The Ancient House, opposite the church, was the home of the writer Oliver Sandys (1892-1964) from 1950 until her death. She used the area as the setting for her book *Quaint Place* (1952). Turn left at the first crossroads into a narrow lane at the side of J.A. Keenan, Grocers and follow this over the railway to the A49. Turn right along the footpath on this side of the road towards a 'P' sign. But don't go quite that far, cross the road, with care, into the lane opposite and walk towards the cottages. Fork left at Knoll Cottage, as signposted 'Public Footpath Ragdon'. Go through the first gate, which opens, and over the next, waymarked, stile. Go straight ahead at the waymarked post at the top of the slope and, beyond the ridge, join another grassy track dipping slightly downhill to the right. Go through the next gate and bear left, still on a grassy track. Before the next field gate, turn right up the slope to find a stile at the top of the facing fence. Go over and continue straight ahead to a stile in the far left-hand corner. At the lane turn right.

Follow the lane to the crossroads at Acton Scott. Turn left for the Farm Museum, which is about five minutes away, on the right-hand side.

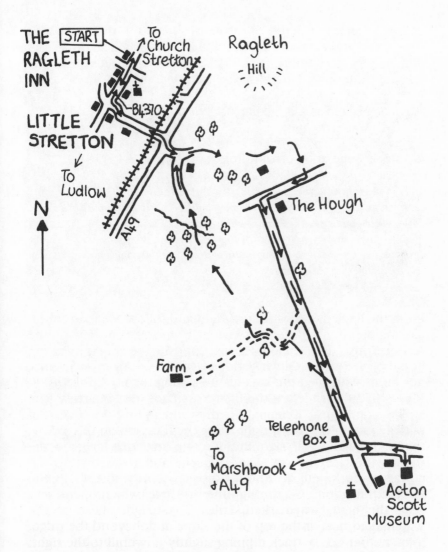

Telephone 01694 781306 for details.

Return from the museum by the same lane, turning right at the crossroads back towards Ragdon. Walk along the lane as far as the first field gate on the left – there is a public footpath sign here. Go through the gate and bear away from the road in the direction in which the arm of the signpost is pointing. On breasting the higher part of the field, you will see below you in

Little Stretton church.

the far left-hand corner, between the trees, the next waymarked stile. Beyond that you join a soggy track, which turns left to a gate with a waymarked stile alongside. Continue ahead to the next gate, now visible on top of the rise a few yards ahead and, crossing the next waymarked stile, turn right. You now walk north-west, with the hedge close on your right through five fields. There is a lovely view from the third field. The Longmynd is directly ahead and its deep valley indentations can be clearly seen. The valley in front of you is Ashes Hollow, while to the left of this is Callow Hollow. Nearer to you, on your right, is Ragleth Hill. On entering the fifth field by another waymarked stile, keep close to the hedge to find the narrow gully which leads into the woods. Crossing the stream by a plank bridge, go straight ahead (not left) and, when the fence on your right ends, fork right to the stile you will now see just above you. Turn left down the new track to return to Knoll Cottage, and from there retrace your steps back to the start.

14 Longville in the Dale
The Longville Arms

There has been an inn on this site since 1793, when it was built to serve the cattle market opposite, now long gone. Also long gone is the railway – the inn was a useful place to wait for trains, which were few and far between. Inside, the Longville Arms is very comfortable, with a nice homely atmosphere.

Among the drinks you will find Carling Black Label, M&B Mild, Bass Special Bitter, Murphy's Irish Stout, Worthington Best Bitter, and Autumn Gold cider. The menu is large and the helpings copious. Steak, Cajun spicy chicken and chicken Kiev, pork, plaice, sole and salmon steaks, lasagne and a variety of salads are all listed, as well as starters and sweets. A daily specials board makes further suggestions. There is also a children's menu. On Monday to Saturday the inn is open from 11 am to 3 pm and 7 pm to 11 pm, and on Sunday from 12 noon to 3 pm and 7 pm to 10.30 pm.

Telephone: 01694 771206.

How to get there: From Shrewsbury drive south on the A49 to Church Stretton and turn left onto the B4371. Longville is midway between Church Stretton and Much Wenlock.

Parking: There is plenty of space in front of the pub.

Length of the walk: 3 miles. Map: OS Landranger 137, Ludlow, Wenlock Edge and surrounding area, or 138 Kidderminster and Wyre Forest area (inn GR 539938).

The walk climbs on an easy gradient from Longville in the valley up and over Wenlock Edge to the famous landmark of Wilderhope Manor. Now in the care of the National Trust, the Manor is used by the YHA as a youth hostel and is sometimes open to the public. This is an easy route. The lane outward is very quiet and drivers considerate to walkers. There is a nice view from the lane towards the Stretton Hills to the west.

The Walk
From the inn bear left towards the signpost at the junction of roads and follow the arm 'Much Wenlock B4371'. Pass the farm and in a few yards turn right into a quiet side lane, marked 'Wilderhope Manor 1½'. The lane crosses the track bed of the former railway, which ran from Craven Arms to Much Wenlock and closed in April 1951. No trace of the track bed now remains. The lane then runs through a cutting and on the left you can see the rock from which Wenlock Edge is formed. Quarries are still working further along the Edge towards Much Wenlock.

At the top of the hill the vehicular entrance to Wilderhope is passed on the left. Continue down the lane a little further to the first field gate on your left. There is a stile on one side of the gate and a bridleway sign. Go over the stile and, keeping the hedge on your right, go ahead through two fields. Go over the stile into the third field and head across towards the far right-hand corner, passing a wooden electricity pylon, to find the field gate, with a stile on the right. Cross over and turn left along a well-defined grassy track towards Wilderhope Manor.

The Manor was built by Thomas Smallman, a major in the king's army during the Civil War, and it is he who still haunts the house and the land around. Several people claim to have seen him and have described his dress in some detail. The

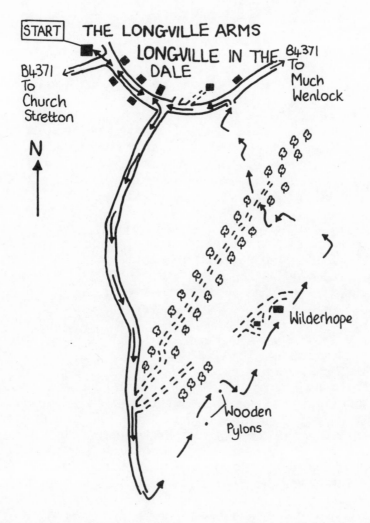

START

THE LONGVILLE ARMS

LONGVILLE IN THE DALE

B4371 To Much Wenlock

B4371 To Church Stretton

N

Wilderhope

Wooden Pylons

sightings have always been by day. The ghost seems friendly, even raising his hand in greeting to a guest at the Manor who saw the major walk across one of the rooms. On another occasion two people in a car saw a horseman in the dress of a Royalist officer riding a horse along the Wenlock Edge road. They thought him real and only realised what they had seen after he had galloped, silently, away. On the OS map you will see marked (further north-east), 'Major's Leap', which is also to do with Major Smallman who, pursued by Roundheads, rode his horse over the edge as the only means of escape. The horse was killed but the major survived by clinging to the branch of a tree to break his fall.

Arriving at the Manor (open to the public on Wednesday to Saturday, 2 pm to 4.30 pm, from April to September, and on Saturdays only from October to March) cross to the right, downhill, over a wide, triangular grassy patch, with the moat wall in front of you. I don't know that it was actually a moat wall, but it has all the appearance of having been one. In the bottom corner of the field, in front of the Manor, is another waymarked gate. Follow the track beyond it. This then joins another one coming from behind the Manor to your left. Now walk on along the new track, which is part of the Shropshire Way. There is a buzzard sign on the first gate post as you join it.

At the end of the first field, cross a stile and then turn left up the field, with the hedge on your left. At the top, turn left through a wicket gate, and immediately turn right over a stile marked with the yellow footpath waymark. Now turn hard right again as the path doubles back a few yards with the fence on your right. The path soon turns to the left and begins a short but steep descent. Being on clay it can be slippery if wet, so take care. There are a few nettles, but nothing to cause a problem. Halfway down cross over a wider track and continue downhill again to find a concealed stile on the edge of a field. Cross the field, still heading in the same direction, to the next stile, which is where the wire fence from the higher part of the field and a hedge from the lower meet. Go over this stile, also waymarked, and turn hard left, as the arrow shows. At the bottom of the field join a track and there is another waymark telling you to turn right.

Passing cars along the road will probably have alerted you to its presence and there is another stile to cross here. Turn left and walk along the road over the old railway bridge – it's only a few yards – back to the village. The former railway station is now a private house and may be seen from the bridge. It isn't the building by the side of the road, although that certainly looks as if it was once the station, but the real one was at the other end of the drive.

15 Bridgnorth
The Bear

This 17th-century inn nestles under the shadow of the North Gate, the sole surviving medieval gate in the town, once one of five. Since its inception in 1640 the Bear has always been an inn and, given that the town walls previously marked the limit of the built up area, must rank as one of the earliest buildings beyond the walls. The inn used to brew its own ales and Bridgnorth beers were reputed to be the second strongest in England, with a gravity of 1060. Both bars are spacious and very comfortable, and the walls are bedecked with framed antique posters. There is a small garden at the back with tables.

The real ales on offer are Batham Bitter and Mild, Boddingtons, Ruddles Best and changing guests, such as Timothy Taylor Landlord, Theakston XB, Holden's Special or Exmoor Gold. Also on draught are Westons cider, Murphy's Irish Stout, Guinness, Foster's, and Miller Pilsner. Food is served at lunchtimes from Monday to Saturday and includes soup, salads, steak and kidney pie, ploughman's lunches, home-

baked ham, and salmon and ginger fish cakes, all home-made and there is a daily specials board. The Bear is open on weekdays from 10.30 am to 3 pm and 5.15 pm to 11 pm, and on Sunday from 12 noon to 2.30 pm and 7 pm to 10.30 pm.
Telephone: 01746 763250.

How to get there: From Shrewsbury take the A458 south-east through Much Wenlock to Bridgnorth. Turn into the town at the start of the bypass and, passing the Rover garage on the right continue straight ahead into Whitburn Street, with the church ahead. Turn left along High Street, under the arch into Northgate, and the Bear is now on your left.

Parking: There is a car park at the rear of the pub. Access is through the filling station on the left at the end of the terrace, between the terrace and the hospital.

Length of the walk: 2 miles. Map: OS Landranger 138 Kidderminster and Wyre Forest area (inn GR 716935).

This is a town walk and is suitable for pushchairs. Bridgnorth is stuffed full of history, with quiet back streets of great beauty and attractive town houses. The parish church of St Leonards and the castle are among its many ancient attractions, while the Severn Valley Railway is of more recent origin. If you want to look in more detail at this fascinating town, guided tours are available from the information centre in Listley Street (telephone: 01746 763358).

The Walk
Turn right out of the pub to the North Gate. The archway to the right was made early this century – before that it was a prison cell, part of the town gaol which extended behind the row of houses to the right. There was a moat this side of the arch. Cross the road into Moat Street, a very picturesque street leading to the church. Outside number 3 note two rings on each side of the road. These rings were put there in 1940, their purpose being to have anti-tank barriers, covered with barbed wire, attached to them. The town walls ran along the right-hand side of the street, but, being only made of oak, were at their weakest point here, and at the end of the street, where the present wall ends, the Parliamentarians broke through in 1646. They then

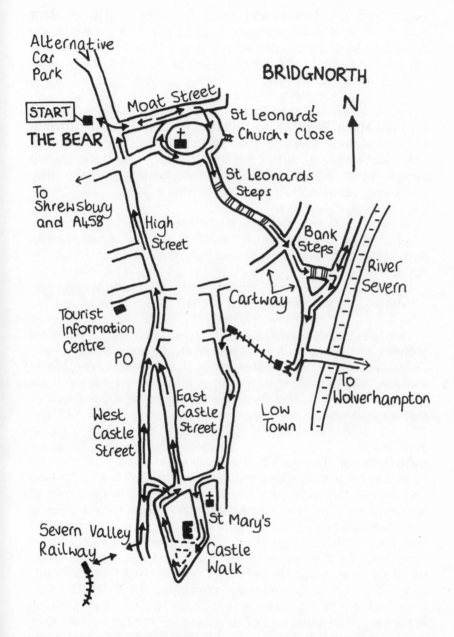

used the church to store their gunpowder and arms and as the building already contained the woodwork from the demolished town hall the result was inevitable when the Royalists, who had retreated to the castle, fired well-aimed incendiaries at the church roof. The resultant explosion sent showers of burning timbers far and wide and so began the great fire of Bridgnorth, which levelled the town.

Now walk round the back of the church, passing Granary Steps. The brick building with three doorways in St Leonard's Close is the 17th-century grammar school. The half-timbered building is Palmers Hospital. These almshouses date from 1687 and were rebuilt in 1889 – only the gate posts are from the original building. To the right of Church Street is Richard Baxter's House, the home of the famous Puritan preacher and one-time curate. St Leonard's church is built on the highest part of the town. It was originally constructed before 1250, but this building in red sandstone is almost entirely Victorian.

Now descend St Leonard's Steps to Cartway, which was once the only route for wheeled vehicles from the riverside docks at Low Town to High Town. The building on the left, with the flat veranda before the front door, was once one of Bridgnorth's 300 public houses and it was here the navvies, building the railway tunnel under the town, would meet to drink away their cares and troubles after a hard day's work. The houses on the right, going up the hill, are built into the cliff face. Descend Cartway to turn left, opposite number 21, and go down Bank Steps. You are now in Low Town. The building at the foot of the steps is, as you can easily see, built into the cliff. Note the two vents coming out of the cliff face just to the right of the building – these are air vents for the kitchen and bathroom! There was a complete terrace of houses here at one time, which accounts for the brick face to the cliff. These were the back walls of the houses and the round hole shows where the cross beams were fitted. Turning to the river, it was here that the sailing ships and barges were moored in the days when Bridgnorth was an important inland port. Sugar was the principal cargo, brought from Bristol, and the roadway was known as Sugar Bag Lane until 1877.

Turn right, with the river on your left, and rejoin Cartway. The house at the corner is Bishop Percy's House. Built in 1580,

Bishop Percy's house.

it was one of the few timber-framed houses to escape the fire. It is named after the Reverend Dr Percy, Bishop of Dromore, Ireland, who was born here in 1729. Now continue down Cartway and along Underhill Street. The bridge across the river was built in 1823 by Thomas Telford, on the site of a former Saxon bridge. Turn right up a narrow alley and journey to High Town the easy way by the cliff railway. At the top, turn left along Castle Walk. The outlook is superb and you may get some idea as to why it was chosen as a site for the castle, for it commanded a view all around, and don't forget that you are at ground level whereas the castle walls would have towered high above you, thus giving an even better viewpoint than we have today.

Turn right up the steps into St Mary's churchyard. The church, like the bridge below, is also the work of Thomas Telford. Just beyond the church turn left along a footpath towards the castle ruins. Built between 1098 and 1101, the remains now lean at an angle of about 15 degrees, greater than the tower of Pisa. It was left in this state after the Civil War, when the Roundheads blew it up. Note the iron hooks on the west side of the tower – on these, mattresses were hung to cushion the impact of cannon balls. The area covered by the castle and its inner sanctum was larger than one would think, encompassing the gardens, the church and the length of East Castle Street beyond the main gate.

If you wish to visit the Severn Valley Railway, turn left at the main gate, just beyond the statue of the goddess Sabrina, and go left along West Castle Street, the road close by, to find the suspension bridge across to the station. You can rejoin the walk afterwards, either by retracing your steps to the statue, or by walking northwards up West Castle Street, to the junction with East Castle Street.

After walking around the gardens, and near the statue, walk back towards the church and turn left into East Castle Street.

The Governor's House is on the right-hand side of East Castle Street and outside it there is a conduit, the town's only source of fresh water until 1946. Between the TSB and the post office was the Barbican, the main entrance to the castle grounds from the north. There is a plaque over the letterbox outside the post office. Beyond the Barbican is High Street, dominated by the Town Hall. The street was originally much wider but buildings on both sides have been built out into it. The Town Hall's pillars are of red sandstone covered with bricks by the Victorians. This does spoil the building somewhat, but, on the other hand, red sandstone is very susceptible to weathering and the brick facing has helped to preserve it. The buildings on the right, past the Town Hall, do not have the extended frontages as do those before it. At the end of High Street is the North Gate – note the plaque over the right-hand archway. Over the sports shop on your left you can just make out the words 'Fire Station'. The first fire engine in the town was bought in 1666, the same year as the Great Fire of London, and housed here. Go through the arch and you are back at the Bear.

16 Aston Munslow
The Swan

The attractive, partly half-timbered Swan inn is at the centre of the hamlet of Aston Munslow. Built in 1600 as a simple and unpretentious farmhouse, parts of the original building can still be seen, for what were once the outside walls now form the inside rooms. Both bars are original, only the rooms branching off them being additions, and the hearth in the rear bar has an oven, indicating that it was formerly a kitchen. The large, very comfortable lounge also started life as a kitchen added to the original house, probably around 1691, the date stated on the cast-iron fireback in the hall.

As for drinks, Bass, Worthington Best Bitter, Carling Black Label, Guinness, Highgate Dark and Dry Blackthorn cider are all on offer. The food includes home-made soup, shepherd's pie or similar, fish, scampi, steak, sausage, egg and chips, jacket potatoes, beefburgers, sandwiches, pizzas, a roast on Sunday, and there are vegetarian and children's menus. Opening hours are 12 noon to 3 pm and 6.30 pm to 11 pm on weekdays, and

12 noon to 3 pm and 7 pm to 10.30 pm on Sundays. No food is available on Monday lunchtimes.

Telephone: 01584 841271.

How to get there: Aston Munslow is on the B4368 road, between Craven Arms and Much Wenlock. From Shrewsbury take either the A49 south and turn left at Craven Arms, or the A458 south-east and turn second right at Much Wenlock onto the B4378.

Parking: There is a small public car park opposite the inn.

Length of the walk: 2½ miles. Map: OS Landranger 137 Ludlow, Wenlock Edge and surrounding area, or 138 Kidderminster and Wyre Forest area (inn GR 512867).

The attractions of this walk are the wonderful views. Corvedale is a rich farming valley, flat and wide, and from the slopes on either side one gets these superb vistas. The early part of this route and later the path near the black barn are the finest viewpoints in the area.

The Walk

From the inn take the lane leading away from the main road. Pass two bungalows on the right and then, at a junction of five roads, turn left. Walk for about 10 yards and find a footpath on the right, the signpost for which is on the left of the lane, which leads towards a house called Arbourdale. Follow this track past Arbourdale and now it begins to swing right. Here, keep close to the hedge on a grassy path, which rises slightly, goes straight ahead and ends at a waymarked stile. Go across the field to a facing field gate, cross the lane and continue ahead through a second field gate. The wall surrounding Aston Hall is on your right. Go through the next gate and bear half-right in the direction of the waymark arrow. Cross the stile on the other side of the field. Now go over the field straight ahead to find a stile in the hedgerow. At first sight it appears to be a double one, but the second stile is on the opposite side of a sunken track. Descend into this and turn right.

The track was clearly a route of some importance in ancient times. On the Ordnance Survey map its route can be traced for many miles. With the coming of the turnpike roads in the valley

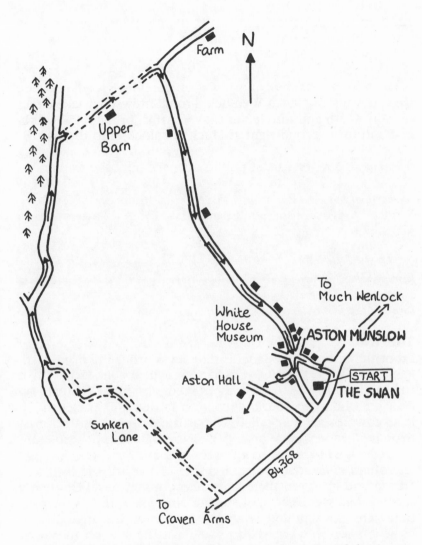

it fell out of use and now remains as a monument of the cross-country ways once heavily used in medieval times, when keeping to the high ground was so important in order to avoid the wet valley bottoms.

After twisting and turning with the track, and perhaps pushing aside some nettles in summer, you emerge finally on a quiet country lane. Turn right and follow this as far as Aston

Aston Munslow.

Top. Here bear right onto a wide, sandy track with a bridleway sign and the blue arrow on the post. Follow the track uphill for ½ mile until level with the black barn across to your right. Turn right through a wide space where previously a gate would have been and follow the track past the barn. It is from here that the best views are found. The hill the other side of the valley is Brown Clee, the summit marked by a radio beacon. The hill to the right is Titterstone Clee, marked with a mushroom-shaped radar mast. One of the international air routes from America to London passes over here, and the contrails of high flying airliners can frequently be seen. When you come to the lane turn right and follow it downhill and back to the start.

As you near the centre of Aston Munslow you will see on your right the entrance gate to the 13th-century White House, a rural museum established in the 1970s by the late owner. Admittance is now only by prior arrangement. (Write to: The Director, The Landmark Trust, Shottesbrooke, Maidenhead, Berks SL6 3SW.) Continue down the lane to the junction of five roads, the lane back to the inn being in front, slightly left of centre.

17 Burwarton
The Boyne Arms

Burwarton is an ancient and stately village looking out on richly wooded slopes and a magnificent panorama of fields. The beautiful old coaching inn, the Boyne Arms, gets its name from the Boyne family, the local landowners. Purpose-built around 1840, it sits at the foot of the magnificent Brown Clee Hill, the highest point in Shropshire, where it is possible to walk for hours looking out over the patchwork of farmland. Here is one of the most impressive entrances of any inn that I have come across. Inside, the lounge bar is spacious and very comfortable.

Tennent's Extra, Bass, Worthington Best Bitter, Carling Black Label, Guinness, Caffrey's Irish Ale, M&B Mild and a guest beer are all on offer, as well as Autumn Gold and Dry Blackthorn ciders. The extensive menu runs to lasagne, home-made chicken and ham pie, gammon, cod, plaice, chicken curry, ploughman's lunches, and various vegetarian dishes, also children's portions and traditional Sunday lunches. Accommodation is available, too. The opening hours are 11 am

to 3 pm and 6 pm to 11 pm on weekdays, and 12 noon to 3 pm and 7 pm to 10.30 pm on Sundays.
    Telephone: 0174 633214.

How to get there: From Shrewsbury you would have to go to either Bridgnorth or Ludlow. From the Bridgnorth direction, turn right at the first roundabout on the bypass on the B4364 towards Ludlow. If approaching from Ludlow, turn left at the first roundabout on the bypass, the A4117 towards Kidderminster, then left again on the B4364. Burwarton is almost midway between the two towns.

Parking: In front of the inn, or in the stable yard.

Length of the walk: 4½ miles. Map: OS Landranger 138 Kidderminster and Wyre Forest area (inn GR 617851).

It is difficult to believe, in such beautiful surroundings and so quiet a backwater as this, that these hills were once a thriving industrial area. Coal was mined and stone quarried where sheep and walkers roam and where the only sound now is the call of the hilltop birds. The scenery from Abdon Burf, once the site of a fortified Roman settlement, is beyond description.

The Walk

Starting from the pub's car park, turn your back on the road and make your way through the narrow passage between the pub and the stable barn. Cross the track ahead to the facing field gate and, entering the park of Boyne Hall, turn left alongside the hedge. On joining the drive to the house, continue ahead, soon crossing a cattle grid. Continue past the farm entrance, on your left, and, after passing through a wooded area, you come to a junction of metalled tracks with a grassy triangle in the middle. Turn left now and follow the track which passes above and behind the farm and then bends to the right before entering a hairpin bend. At the bend, go ahead through a field gate with a fire sign on one side and follow a well-defined muddy track which bears slightly left uphill. Near the top of the field the track draws near to a fence along the other side of the field on your left. Bear away right now, keeping to the right of the tree-topped hump ahead.

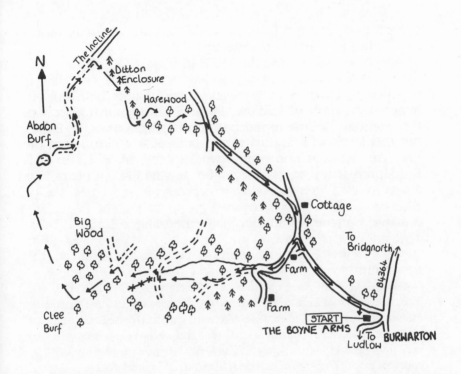

To your right, and below you, you can hear the sound of the stream in the valley and across the other side there is a fern-covered slope dotted with trees. As you come alongside the hump, you will reach a wide, grassy path cut into the ledge of the hillside. Follow this until it joins a crossing track further on. Go across the track to the gate nearly opposite and continue uphill. There is a fence on your left, but the exact path here is not important. When the fence on the left turns away left, turn right to what at first appears to be a gate. Climb over and turn left along a well-defined forest track, which ends at a field gate by the trees. Go through. You are now on the high ground with views all round, but this is only the start. You have to reach the summit on which stands the television relay station clearly visible from here. From the gate bear right across a grassy area, bearing away from the wall, and with rough grass to your right. The gate ahead is marked with a Shropshire Way buzzard sign.

Beyond the gate are two grassy tracks. Ignoring the track going left alongside the fence, take the other one which climbs slightly, with a bank and ditch on the right-hand side.

This bank and ditch are not accidental but serve to mark the boundary between two parishes – this is common on the Shropshire Hills. If you look left you can see, below on the lower ground, the outline of the ancient hill fort of Nordy Bank. Drawing level with the fence again, continue ahead with it on your left. Nearing the relay station, the fence turns left and drops away downhill. There is a soggy, muddy path here and if you look to your left there is another Shropshire Way sign fixed on the sixth post down, on what appears to be a stile. But you turn right now and follow a rather wet path to the relay station. The base of the Ordnance Survey triangulation point makes a welcome seat and from here you have the 360 degree view I promised you.

Arthur Mee, in his book *The King's England* claims you can see 15 counties on a clear day, but can we . . . let's see. To the south-east, the humpy hills of the Malverns straddle the borders of Worcestershire and Herefordshire and, beyond, there is the low, flat outline of the Cotswolds, Gloucestershire. To the south-west, the Sugar Loaf near Abergavenny, Gwent (Monmouthshire), the Black Mountains and the Brecon Beacons, formerly Brecknock and to the north is Radnor Forest, Radnorshire. West of the Longmynd is Long Mountain, Montgomeryshire and on a very clear day you can see, further west, Plynlimmon, Cardiganshire and to the north of that the lumpy outline of Cader Idris, Merionethshire. To the north-west the mountains of North Wales can be seen, Denbighshire. To the north is the Shropshire Plain, which formerly merged with part of Flint near Whitchurch but still does merge with Cheshire. To the north-east Cannock Chase, Staffordshire – which makes 14! I have read that on a clear day from the Longmynd it is possible to see Snowdon, Caenarvonshire, so it should be possible from here as well, and that would make 15.

From the summit, descend to the metalled track and turn right. Follow the track downhill, passing the ruins of an old stone-crushing plant. Shortly afterwards, to your left, you will see a stone-walled cutting, now grassed over, where once ran a railway line to the crushing plant, while a few steps further, and

The abandoned quarry at Abdon Burf.

again on your left, are the remains of two railway rails upended in the ground and, nearby, several old timber sleepers. At the bend in the road you join The Incline, from where the mineral wagons were hauled up and down the 1 in 2 incline to Ditton Priors railway. At the bend, on your left, the line levels out to end at the remains of the winding house. Walk on down the road as far as the cattle grid.

Turn right now and follow a level, grassy path along the side of the woods, with a fence on your left. After ¼ mile, turn through the first gate on the left and follow a well-defined track which zig-zags downhill through the woods to emerge at a five-bar gate. Turn right and at the fork of tracks just ahead, go left by a post with '5' engraved on it. This is part of the forest trail and the posts indicate points of interest. At the junction of estate roads at the foot of the hill, just before an estate cottage, turn right. There is a very welcome seat on the right for weary limbs. Continue ahead, over the cattle grid, just beyond which is the junction of estate roads by the grassy triangle which you met on the outward leg, so from here retrace your steps back past the farm to the pub.

(18) Alveley
The Three Horse Shoes

The Three Horse Shoes is right in the middle of the village of Alveley, which is situated on the east bank of the river Severn. The pub is the oldest licensed public house in Shropshire and dates from 1406. The lounge bar is capacious, homely and comfortable, with a wide fireplace, recently restored. Oak beams line the ceiling and horse brasses the walls. The inn once served the drove road, which ran alongside and was at one time the main road from Bridgnorth to Kidderminster, until the coming of the turnpike road, now the A442, around 1840. After that, the opening of Alveley coal mine in 1934 made it into the miners' pub and the centre of village affairs until the mine closed in 1969.

Harp lager, Marston's Pedigree, Kronenbourg 1664 and Banks's Bitter and Mild are on offer, as well as Scrumpy Jack cider. There is a nice garden and a children's play area with a climbing frame and swings. The menu lists a wide range of starters, hot or cold sandwiches, ploughman's lunches, salads

and pastas. The main dishes include pheasant, a comprehensive selection of steaks and chicken and fish dishes. There is also an excellent take-away service of appetising hot meals. Food is available from 12 noon to 2 pm and 7 pm to 9 pm. The pub is open from 12 noon to 3 pm every day and from 7 pm to 11 pm on weekdays, 7 pm to 10.30 pm on Sunday.
Telephone: 01746 780642.

How to get there: From Shrewsbury drive south-east on the A458 through Much Wenlock as far as the Bridgnorth bypass, turning right at the second roundabout, onto the A442 Kidderminster road. Some 8 miles south turn right at the signpost for Alveley and the Severn Valley Country Park. The inn is at the T-junction in the centre of the village.

Parking: There is a good car park in the inn yard.

Length of the walk: 3½ miles. Map: OS Landranger 138 Kidderminster and Wyre Forest area (inn GR 760845).

You have two options on this walk. You can either stroll along the bank of the river Severn or cross on the ferry from Hampton Loade and travel to Highley, the village on the other side of the river, by steam train. The walk is easy, quiet and very enjoyable. There is little or no traffic at all on the lane to the Butter Cross and from the river bank you can watch the trains on the other side.

The Walk
Turn left out of the pub yard and walk towards the church. St Mary's was built in 1140 of the local red sandstone, much used in building work here in the centre of the village. At the road junction with the sign 'Butter Cross, Circular route', turn right. The cottage on the corner was formerly the post office.

Opposite the church is the Sun Inn, where it is reputed that Oliver Cromwell stayed, leaving his horses in the church vestry. Walk now along a quiet, winding lane with pleasant fields on either side. Shortly after passing Yew Tree Cottage, the last of two isolated cottages on the right-hand side, the road bends to the left. Here you will find the Butter Cross.

The name is probably a corruption of 'Bartering Cross' from

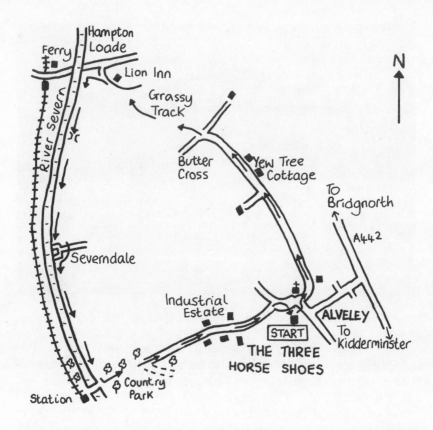

the time when it was used during the plague, when food would be left here for the villagers at Alveley after the village was struck by the Black Death in 1349. But the cross is much more ancient than this – probably it is a 10th-century praying cross, for it is considered to be 100 years older than the church. Its origins are obscure but it seems that monks on their way to and from Wenlock Abbey would have used it before the church was built.

Walk straight on now along the grassy track and through a facing gate into a field. With the ruins of red-brick barns to your left, go straight ahead on the 'level' ground, which drops gently downhill and bends to the left. A thicker hedge will soon be found on your left and a caravan site then comes into view. At the bottom corner, between the hedge and the caravan site, is

The old post office at Alveley.

a stile. Cross the stile into the Lion Inn car park.

Go straight ahead, passing the inn on your right. At the end of the car park find a narrow footpath to your left. It begins by the gate with the notice 'Anglers No Parking' on it, and a public footpath sign pointing the wrong way!

If you wish to travel to Highley by train, stay on the pub road and turn left to cross the river by the ferry. If the ferry is not this side, ring the bell. The station is straight up the lane on the other side.

The footpath from the pub car park terminates at the river bank and here you turn left onto the riverside path. The name 'Loade' signifies a place where river barges would load up with their cargoes of coal to take down river. The path now crosses five fields by stiles or footbridges until you come to Severndale, a red-brick building on the river bank. The path here swings left round the corner of the field to the stile which is 20 yards up the field away from the river. Cross the lane beyond it and go over the next stile. The path now crosses a parkland-like field, with the wall of Severndale to your right. Skirt round a wooded area to rejoin the river bank and continue ahead through three more fields. The bridge to Highley is now in view and crossing the last stile, go through a wooded area to join the track which crosses the bridge. Turn left.

If you came by train to Highley, walk from the station down to the river bank and turn left to the bridge – anyone at the station will give you directions.

At the end of the track from the bridge is a country park signpost. Don't follow the arm pointing to the visitor centre, but use the other track just across to the left, still walking with the bridge to your back. This track soon leaves the country park and, passing the rather derelict industrial estate, turn right at the road junction to return to Alveley. Note the red-sandstone walls and buildings as you near the village again.

19 **Purslow**
The Hundred House

The sign at the Hundred House is well worth studying. It shows a courtroom with magistrates, plaintiff, defendant and witnesses, and portrays the inn as it was originally, for a hundred house is the ancient name for a court house. It was later converted into a coaching inn and tradition has it that a Bishop of Hereford, en route from his castle at Bishop's Castle, would stop here to change horses and refresh. The building was once part of the Powis estate, the house for which is the nearby Walcot Hall. The inn was sold by the estate in 1910 when the Powis family moved from Walcot to Powis Castle at Welshpool. Now a freehouse, the pub is very comfortable. It has a separate dining area and there is also a large garden with outside tables.

The lunchtime menu consists of various fish dishes, including plaice, cod, scampi, gammon, Texas-style beef, Cajun chicken, as well as baked potatoes, salads, and ploughman's lunches and vegetarian dishes. In the evenings, in addition to the bar food, there is also a more extensive dinner menu. Sunday lunchtime sees the traditional roast, but booking in advance is essential. Ansells Mild and Bitter, Tetley Bitter, Guinness, Lowernbräu and Skol lagers and Woodpecker and Strongbow ciders are served, alongside Liebfraumilch and vin de pays white wines, on draught. On Monday the pub is open in the evening only, and on Tuesday to Friday the hours are 12 noon to 3 pm and 7 pm to 11 pm, or all day if there is the demand. On Saturday it opens from 12 noon to 11 pm, and the Sunday hours are 12 noon to 3 pm and 7 pm to 10.30 pm.

Telephone: 01588 660541.

How to get there: Purslow is on the B4368 road from Craven Arms to Clun. From Shrewsbury drive south on the A49 through Church Stretton and turn right in Craven Arms onto the Clun road. Purslow occupies more room on the map than it does on the ground for it consists only of a farm, the Hall, and the pub, the latter being easy to find on the left-hand side of the road – you can't possibly miss it.

Parking: There are two car parks, one in front of the pub, and the other at the back, the entrance to which is hard left at the inn sign.

Length of the walk: 3 miles. Map: OS Landranger 137 Ludlow, Wenlock Edge and surrounding area (inn GR 360809).

This is effectively two walks joined together. As you will see from the map, in addition to the circuit described, you can choose either the first part to the west and back, or the second part to Clunbury and back. The two halves are around 1½ miles each. This walk gave me great pleasure – it's easy, it's level, and it's quiet. In 1994 the county council erected new stiles and signposts everywhere in the area and with the waymarks, the route is very easy to find. You follow the wide valley of the river Clun, crossing grassy fields, and being on the level throughout makes the walk suitable for all ages. This quiet corner of Shropshire is almost entirely unknown and the peace and tranquillity guaranteed!

The Walk
Turn left from the pub and walk down the lane for a few yards to bear right at the footpath sign, through a galvanised wicket

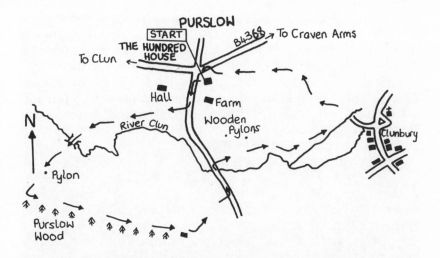

gate. Go straight ahead across a large field, but not close to the wall on the right, which is the boundary around Purslow Hall. Gradually make your way ahead and downhill, but not sharply downhill, heading to a flat area at the far end of the field. Go through the facing gate and fork half-left across the second field to the footbridge which is now visible. Cross over the river Clun and go straight ahead, slightly right, to the stile a few yards up the field on the right-hand side. Cross the stile and turn left, with the hedge on the left, and go up the field, passing the wooden electricity pylon, to another stile at the top between the field gate and the cottage.

Turn left along the lane on the edge of Purslow Wood. Shortly after passing Ashbeds cottage, turn left at a bridleway sign, through a field gate, and cross two fields, with the hedge on your right, to reach the road again.

Turn left along the road, towards the bridge. Cross the bridge and just after it turn right over another stile with a footpath sign. Go straight ahead. Leaving the stream away to your right, head towards a white building visible in the far distance. Passing to the right of the second wooden electricity pylon, head towards a double pylon by which, just to the right of the field gate, is another stile. In the second field bear right, close now to the river again, and you will find that a third stile comes into view. Cross this and go straight ahead through the third field, through

Clunton village.

a field gate, and cross a fourth field, heading towards the white railings of a footbridge by which access may be made to Clunbury village.

It is well worth the effort of the extra few yards to visit Clunbury. What is it that A.E. Housman says about it in the immortal poem of his?

'Clunton and Clunbury, Clungunford and Clun,
Are the quietest places under the sun.'

Indeed it is so, even to this day. Although it was midday when I last did this walk not a living soul was to be seen and it is like this whenever I come here. There are no shops, pubs or garages, just a few attractive half-timbered cottages gathered around the church, built on the highest point.

Now return to the footbridge and, going through the galvanised wicket gate again, bear right, as waymarked, across the first field, passing between two wooden pylons to the next galvanised wicket gate. In the second field, follow the hedge on your right, and get to the right of a ditch by the driest means possible, for the next stile is on the other side of this ditch in the first corner of the field. Cross the stile and turn left in the third field to the waymarked field gate just ahead. The fourth field is a big one and you go straight ahead, bearing slightly right, as the waymark indicates, heading towards the red-brick house in the distance. The way out of the field is in the corner by the house – there is a waymark on a post just before a stile. Cross the stile and you will find yourself in the back garden of the house! Bear slightly left through the trees, behind the red-brick garage to the tarmac drive. Opposite the back door is a flight of four stone steps set in the bank and above them a wicket gate, which leads into the orchard. Bear slightly right in the orchard towards a line of cypress trees and the last stile will be seen between the trees. Turn left in the road, to reach the pub, which is next door.

20 Bromfield
The Clive Arms

Bromfield gets its name from the time when the fields surrounding it were golden with broom, a low shrub covered with yellow flowers in spring and summer. It stands at the confluence of two rivers, the Teme, which you cross on the walk, beyond the church, and the Onny which passes under the A49 almost opposite the pub. The village is mentioned in the Domesday Book and before then Roman battles were fought. Between the village and the railway, to the north of Station Lane, is a large area known as Roman Camp. Most of the properties in the village form part of the estate of the Earl of Plymouth, who resides at Oakly Park, and it is on the estate that most inhabitants earn their living. The A49 bisects the village now, but formerly it snaked its way through the main part of the village, which is on the west side of the new road. On the opposite side of the main road from the village is the inn, standing on another extinct track of the old road.

The Clive Arms is, as country pubs go, fairly new, as the

present building was only opened as a public house in 1976, the previous pub, which is the adjacent building, having been closed in the early 1900s by the then Lady Plymouth – a most interesting story. The groom at the big house, whose job it was to exercise the horses, always did so by taking them to the pub, where he stayed until drunk. On the occasion which led to its closure, the Plymouths had returned from London and Lady Plymouth ordered her horse to be made ready to take her for a ride, which it did, straight to the pub! On discovering the truth she had the pub closed and it was not re-opened until 1976!

The inn gets its name from Robert Clive, Clive of India, and descendants of his, the Windsor-Clive family, are the local landowners. The building itself dates from the early 19th century. There is a large, comfortable lounge with an open fireplace. Bass, Tennent's Extra, Bass Special, M&B Mild, Murphy's Irish Stout, Carling Black Label and Strongbow and Stowford Press ciders are all on offer. The varied menu includes steak and kidney pie, gammon, cold roast beef, scampi, chicken, plaice, pork sausages, a cheese platter and various rolls and sandwiches. The opening hours are 11.30 am to 2.30 pm (3 pm Saturday and Sunday), and 6.30 pm to 11 pm (10.30 pm Sunday).
Telephone: 01584 77364.

How to get there: Bromfield is 2 miles north of Ludlow on the A49 trunk road. From Shrewsbury drive south on the A49 through Church Stretton and Craven Arms, and Bromfield is 2 miles beyond the level crossing at Onibury.

Parking: There is a large car park at the inn.

Length of the walk: 3½ miles (4½ miles for the longer walk, see map). Map: OS Landranger 137 Ludlow, Wenlock Edge and surrounding area (inn GR 483770).

You will find this a very pleasant and easy walk for a family. The walk is entirely over the Earl of Plymouth's land and much of it on estate roads, but do not let that put you off as the only vehicles allowed are estate vehicles and they are very few and far between. After passing the church and crossing the river Teme, the walk skirts the outside of Oakly Park before bearing off to the south-west to make a circular tour of the outer farms.

The Walk

From the pub turn right on the dead stretch of the former main road, towards the telephone box. The lane which goes to your right is Station Lane, reputedly haunted by the ghost of Mrs Holland, an old lady who lived there until her death in the 1930s, after which many people saw her ghost. It has not, however, been encountered since the sand and gravel workings behind the village were started.

Cross the A49 when safe to do so to the pavement on the opposite side and walk towards the junction with the A4113 Leintwardine/Knighton road. Turn left and left again into a side road heading towards the church. For its size, Bromfield has a disproportionately morbid history. On the pub side of the A49 there is the ghost of Mrs Holland, while on this side of the road was murder done in 1784. The victim was the wife of the mason John Green and was murdered in her cellar while drawing beer from a cask. Her husband was supposedly at Ludlow races at the time and a reward of £50 was offered for the arrest of the villain and, in 1784 £50 was a fortune! John Green's alibi was as full of holes as a colander and he was eventually arrested and taken first to Ludlow gaol and finally to Shrewsbury gaol where he was hanged for the crime.

The church and the nearby gatehouse are all that remains of a former priory. The earliest record of a church here dates back to AD 900, but the oldest parts of the present building date from the 11th century. A religious house was founded here during the reign of Edward the Confessor (1042-1066) and it contained 12 secular canons. In 1135 it became a priory affiliated to the Benedictine Abbey of St Peter at Gloucester. The archway over the entrance at the gatehouse is worth noting.

From the church continue along the estate road, passing on your left the 15th-century priory gatehouse, and then crossing the narrow bridge over the river Teme. Notice the Old Mill, almost lost amongst the encroaching greenery to your left. Ahead, where the roads fork, go straight on, with the lodge gate on your left. The outside of Oakly Park is now on your left and soon Oakly House will be seen across the park. It is of early 18th-century construction in red brick. The main entrance is on the other side and we see from the estate road the back of the building but it is, nonetheless, a quite impressive place even

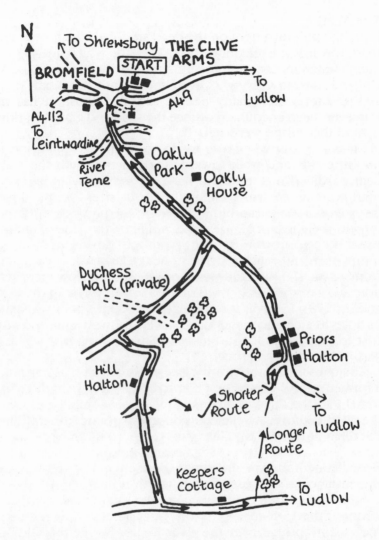

from this distance. The present Earl is the 14th in succession.

Continue along the road to a T-junction. There is a public bridleway signpost here with two blue waymark arrows on it. Turn right in the direction shown by the arm on the post and walk along the new lane for ½ mile. Shortly after passing Duchess Walk and a black Nissen hut, turn left along a rough farm track which takes you to Hill Halton, a black and white half-timbered house. Continue on the track to the left of Hill Halton, after which the way becomes grassy. Ignoring the first bridleway signpost at the end of the garden, continue round the bend just ahead where you will find, near a wooden electricity pylon, a public footpath signpost (it is actually a bridleway, the sign is incorrect!).

For the longer walk (see map) this second signpost points the way, straight on to the estate road, turn left and, after passing the keeper's cottage, turn left at the next gate. There is a stile and an armless footpath post close by.

The shorter route however turns left off the grassy track and the route is indicated on the second signpost by a blue bridleway waymark pointing through the second of two field gates side by side. Go through the right hand of the two gates and walk ahead, with the hedge on your left. Ahead you will soon see the farm buildings at Priors Halton. A narrow section of scrub on your left has been fenced off with barbed wire but this has been removed at the corner of the field, and you can reach the field gate. Go through the gate and by a yellow footpath waymark sign on the fence, turn right down the field, with the hedge on your right. Follow the hedge to the bottom of the field, turning left alongside the stream. Across the field to your left is a row of wooden electricity pylons, the last of which has two cable supports on either side. When you near this find the wooden footbridge across the stream to your right.

The bridge has several footpath waymarks on it. On reaching the other side, turn left around the edge of the field, there is a fence on your left. Follow this to the other end of the field where you exit from the field by a gate and turn left onto a wide, hedged-in, grassy track. It is here the long walk rejoins. Follow the grassy track to the estate road at Priors Halton and turn left. Passing between the farmhouses and barns by a bit of rough road, regain the well-maintained estate road beyond and follow this back to the pub, rejoining the outward walk near Oakly House.